Free Library Enoch Pratt, Edward Stabler

The Enoch Pratt Free Library of Baltimore City

Letters and Documents Relating to its Foundation and Organization....

Free Library Enoch Pratt, Edward Stabler

The Enoch Pratt Free Library of Baltimore City
Letters and Documents Relating to its Foundation and Organization....

ISBN/EAN: 9783337063481

Printed in Europe, USA, Canada, Australia, Japan

Cover: Foto ©ninafisch / pixelio.de

More available books at **www.hansebooks.com**

THE ENOCH PRATT FREE LIBRARY

OF BALTIMORE CITY

LETTERS AND DOCUMENTS RELATING TO ITS
FOUNDATION AND ORGANIZATION

WITH THE

DEDICATORY ADDRESSES AND EXERCISES

JANUARY 4, 1886.

BALTIMORE
1886

TRUSTEES.

ENOCH PRATT,   CHARLES J. BONAPARTE,
GEORGE WM. BROWN,   GEORGE B. COLE,
NATHL. H. MORISON, LL.D.,   EDWARD STABLER, JR.,
HENRY JANES,   JAMES A. GARY,
JOHN W. McCOY.

OFFICERS OF THE BOARD OF TRUSTEES.

ENOCH PRATT, *President.*
GEORGE B. COLE, *Vice-President.*
EDWARD STABLER, JR., *Secretary.*
HENRY JANES, *Treasurer.*

COMMITTEES OF THE BOARD.

Executive Committee.   *Library Committee.*

ENOCH PRATT,   JOHN W. McCOY,
JAMES A. GARY,   NATHL. H. MORISON, LL.D.,
HENRY JANES.   GEORGE B. COLE.

Committee on Accounts.

EDWARD STABLER, JR.,
CHARLES J. BONAPARTE,
GEORGE WM. BROWN.

OFFICERS OF THE LIBRARY.

LEWIS H. STEINER, M. D., *Librarian.*
CHARLES EVANS, *Assist. Librarian.*
HENRY C. WAGNER, *Registrar.*

Press of Isaac Friedenwald, Baltimore.

CONTENTS.

	PAGE
LETTERS:	
From Enoch Pratt to Mayor and City Council,	5
" Hon. Wm. P. Whyte, Mayor, to City Council,	8
" Hon. Wm. P. Whyte, Mayor, to City Council,	10
" The Law Officers of the City to the Mayor,	11
" Hon. Wm. P. Whyte, Mayor, to City Council,	30
" Enoch Pratt to the Board of Trustees,	48
Original Action of the City Council,	9
Action of the City Council Accepting Deed from Enoch Pratt and Wife,	46
Enabling Act Passed by the General Assembly of Maryland,	13
Joint Resolution of Thanks to Enoch Pratt Passed by the General Assembly,	18
Ordinance of the City Council Providing for the Perpetual Annuity, etc.,	20
Ordinance of the City Council Providing for the Investment of the Library Fund,	33
Election by the Citizens of Baltimore to Ratify the Enabling Act and Ordinances,	28
Mayor's Proclamation of the Result of the Election,	29
Deed from Enoch Pratt and Wife to Mayor and City Council,	36
Dedication Ceremonies, January 4, 1886,	51
Programme,	52
Prayer by Rev. Charles R. Weld, B. D.,	53
Address by Hon. James Hodges, Mayor of Baltimore,	55
Response of Enoch Pratt,	68
Oration by the Hon. George Wm. Brown, of the Board of Trustees,	70
Address by Hon. J. Morrison Harris, of Baltimore,	86
" " Hon. F. C. Latrobe, Ex-Mayor of Baltimore,	98
" " Dr. Lewis H. Steiner, Librarian,	101
Description of Central Library Building,	108
" " Branch Library Buildings,	115
Biographical Sketch of Enoch Pratt,	117

LETTER OF ENOCH PRATT.

BALTIMORE, *January* 21, 1882.
*To the Honorable the Mayor and
 City Council of Baltimore.*

I have for some years contemplated establishing a Free Circulating Library, for the benefit of our whole City, and in pursuance of this plan I have entered into a contract to erect a fireproof building on my Mulberry street lot, capable of holding 200,000 volumes—my purpose being to have branches connected with it in the four quarters of the City, under the same management.

The excavation for the foundation has been commenced, and the building will be well advanced this year, and completed in the summer of 1883. It will cost, when ready for occupancy, about two hundred and twenty-five thousand dollars ($225,000), and upon its completion I propose to deed it to the City. The title to all the books and property is to be vested in the City, and I will pay to your Honorable Body, upon its completion, the additional sum of eight hundred and thirty-three thousand three hundred and thirty-three and a third dollars ($833,333⅓), making one million fifty-eight thousand three hundred and thirty-three and one-third dollars, provided the City will grant and create an annuity of fifty thousand dollars ($50,000) per annum forever, payable quarterly to the Board of Trustees, for the support and maintenance of the Library and its branches.

I propose that a Board of nine Trustees be incorporated for the management of "The Pratt Free Library of the City of Baltimore," the Board to be selected by myself from our best citizens, and all vacancies which shall occur, shall be filled by the Board. The articles of incorporation will contain a provision that no Trustee or officer shall be appointed or removed on religious or political grounds. The Trustees are to receive from the City the quarterly payments, and to expend it at their discretion for the purposes of the Library.

It is believed that this annual sum will afford a sufficient fund for the purchase of books, for establishing the branches, and for the general management.

The Trustees will be required to make an annual report to the Mayor and City Council of their proceedings, and of the condition of the Library, and the report will contain a full account of the money received and expended.

This plan is suggested not without due consideration of the power of the City to carry it out. The

City is expressly authorized by its charter to accept trusts "for any general corporation purpose, or for the general purposes of education"; and although its power of creating debts is limited by the Constitution of the State, yet as the property of the Library is to belong to the City, and as it will receive a sum of money to be disposed of as it pleases, with the engagement only to pay an annual sum for the support of its own Institution, it is believed that such a transaction will not involve the creation of a debt within the meaning of the constitutional prohibition.

I suggest that if the money to be paid by me as above stated, were added to the Sinking Fund, and the Interest carefully funded, it would, in no very long time, pay off the debt of the City; but this is intended only as a suggestion, and the disposal of the money is left to your Honorable Body.

If, however, your Honorable Body should, on mature consideration, be of the opinion that the annual payments as proposed would involve the creation of a debt, authority for that may be obtained by complying with the provisions of the Constitution; that is, the debt may be created by the City, provided it be authorized by an act of the General Assembly of Maryland, and by an ordinance of the Mayor and City Council of Baltimore, submitted to the legal voters of the City of Baltimore at such time and place as may be fixed by said ordinance, and approved by a majority of the votes cast at such time and place. I cannot but think that such an authority from the General Assembly, and from the Mayor and City Council of Baltimore, and from a majority of the legal voters of the City, would be cheerfully given.

The plan proposed for the support and management of the Library is the result of long and careful consideration, and, I am satisfied, is well adapted to promote the great object in view, the free circulation of the books of a large and ever-growing Library among the people of the whole City. I trust that it will receive the approval of your Honorable Body, and of the citizens of Baltimore.

ENOCH PRATT.

MAYOR'S OFFICE, CITY HALL,
BALTIMORE, *January* 23, 1882.
To the Honorable the Members of the
First and Second Branches of the City Council,
GENTLEMEN:

I transmit herewith a communication from Enoch Pratt, Esq., dated January 21, 1882, proposing the erection and transfer to the City, for public use, of a Library Building, upon certain terms therein indicated.

The tender of this munificent gift to the City is worthy of all praise, and I commend to your careful consideration the conditions with which the donation is coupled.

Very respectfully yours,
WM. PINKNEY WHYTE,
Mayor.

ACTION OF THE CITY COUNCIL.

BALTIMORE, *January* 31, 1882.

Mr. Wilmer, from the Joint Standing Committee on Ways and Means, submitted the following report and accompanying resolution, which were read:

The Joint Standing Committee on Ways and Means, to whom was referred a communication from Mr. Enoch Pratt in relation to the donation of a Public Library to the City of Baltimore, having given the matter a careful consideration, report favorably thereon, and ask the adoption of the resolution as annexed.

SKIPWITH WILMER,
WM. E. BRODERICK,
D. CALDWELL IRELAND,
First Branch.
D. GIRAUD WRIGHT,
H. G. FLEDDERMAN,
M. E. MOONEY,
Second Branch.

Resolved by the Mayor and City Council of Baltimore that, in behalf of the people of Baltimore, they do gratefully accept the munificent gift of Mr. Enoch Pratt of the sum of $1,058,000, offered by him for the establishment of a Free Public Library.

That Mr. Pratt be requested to have the Trustees whom he proposes to appoint, organize under the name of "The Enoch Pratt Free Library of Baltimore City," so that his name may be inseparably associated with the Institution which he has founded, and the City which will owe so much to his wise generosity.

That the law officers of the City be requested to ascertain what legislation is required to enable the City to accept the trust upon the terms proposed by Mr. Pratt, and to report the same to the City Council, with a draft of the necessary acts or ordinances, at as early a day as possible.

On motion of Mr. Wilmer, the resolution was read a second time, by special order, and adopted.

MAYOR'S OFFICE, CITY HALL,
BALTIMORE, *February* 14, 1882.

To the Honorable the Members of the
First Branch of the City Council,

GENTLEMEN:

In obedience to the terms of the resolution of the Mayor and City Council, approved February 2, 1882,

I transmit to you a communication from the City Counsellor and the City Solicitor, covering a bill for presentation to the Legislature " to enable the Mayor and City Council of Baltimore to accept a donation from Enoch Pratt for the establishment and perpetual endowment of a Free Public Library in said City, to be known as " The Enoch Pratt Free Library of Baltimore City," etc., etc.

As will be observed, the names of the Trustees are not inserted, but are to be presented by Mr. Pratt when the bill is introduced into the Legislature.

Very respectfully,
Your obedient servant,
WM. PINKNEY WHYTE,
Mayor.

LAW DEPARTMENT, CITY HALL,
BALTIMORE, *February* 11, 1882.

HON. W. PINKNEY WHYTE,
Mayor of Baltimore City,

DEAR SIR:

In accordance with the joint resolution of the Mayor and City Council, approved February 2d, instructing the law officers of the City to draft the necessary measures of legislation to enable the City to accept the offer of Mr. Enoch Pratt to found and endow a Free Public Library in this City, we beg leave to submit the accompanying draft of an enabling act, to be passed by the Legislature, such as in our judgment would be required to enable the City to avail itself of Mr. Pratt's offer upon the terms proposed by him. While the draft of a bill submitted herewith will be found, we think, sufficient for this purpose, we are also assured that its provisions accord with the views and wishes of Mr. Pratt.

The blank left in the second section for the names of the Trustees (to be nominated by Mr. Pratt) is designed to be filled after the bill has been introduced into the Legislature. As the passage of the enabling act and the incorporation of the Trustees should properly precede the passage of the ordinance, the terms of which will necessarily have to conform to those of the act as passed by the Legislature, no draft of an ordinance is at present submitted.

Very respectfully,
JAMES L. McLANE,
City Counsellor.
THOMAS W. HALL,
City Solicitor.

ENABLING ACT PASSED BY THE GENERAL ASSEMBLY OF MARYLAND,

January Session, 1882, Chapter 181.

An Act to enable the Mayor and City Council of Baltimore to accept a donation from Enoch Pratt for the establishment and perpetual endowment of a Free Public Library in said City, to be known as "The Enoch Pratt Free Library of Baltimore City," and to provide for the appointment and incorporation of Trustees for the management thereof.

Whereas, Enoch Pratt, of the City of Baltimore, has, with signal generosity, public spirit and philanthropy, offered to establish an institution to be known as "The Enoch Pratt Free Library of Baltimore City," and for that purpose has agreed to erect upon a lot on Mulberry street in said City, owned by him, a Library building, to cost the sum of two hundred and twenty-five thousand dollars, or thereabout, and to convey the said lot and building when completed to the Mayor and City Council of Baltimore; and also to pay the sum of eight hundred and thirty-three thousand three hundred and thirty-three dollars and thirty-three cents to the said Mayor and City Council of Baltimore, provided the said Mayor and City Council will accept said conveyance and said sum of money, and agree by an ordinance to grant and create an annuity and to pay annually to a Board of nine Trustees and their successors the sum of fifty thousand dollars perpetually hereafter forever, in equal quarter-yearly payments, for the purchase and maintenance of the said Library, with not less than four branches in different parts of the City, said branches to be established by said Trustees within such time as can be reasonably accomplished out of said quarterly payments, the title to said Library, its branches, books, and all other property, to be vested in the Mayor and City Council of Baltimore, the control and management of the said Library and other property to be in said Board of Trustees:

And whereas, the plan thus proposed offers the means of perpetually promoting and diffusing knowledge and education among the people of the City of Baltimore, and it is therefore proper that full power should be conferred on the corporation of the Mayor and City Council of Baltimore to avail itself thereof for the purposes aforesaid; therefore:

SECTION 1. Be it enacted by the General Assembly of Maryland that the Mayor and City Council of Baltimore be and they are hereby authorized and empowered to accept the said proposal of the said Enoch Pratt as set forth in the preamble to this act; and full power and authority are hereby given to said Mayor and City Council of Baltimore, upon the conveyance of said lot of ground and the improvements aforesaid, and upon the payment to said Mayor and

City Council by the said Enoch Pratt of said sum of eight hundred and thirty-three thousand three hundred and thirty-three dollars and thirty-three cents, to contract and agree by ordinance, to be approved by the legal voters of said City as hereinafter provided, to pay perpetually forever to the Board of Trustees of "The Enoch Pratt Free Library of Baltimore City," as hereinafter provided for, the sum of fifty thousand dollars per annum in equal quarterly payments forever.

SECTION 2. And be it further enacted that Enoch Pratt, George Wm. Brown, Nathaniel H. Morison, Henry Janes, Charles J. Bonaparte, George B. Cole, Edward Stabler, Jr., James A. Gary, John W. McCoy, and their successors, be and they are hereby constituted and appointed the Board of Trustees of "The Enoch Pratt Free Library of Baltimore City"; and they and their successors are hereby constituted and appointed a body politic and corporate by the name of "The Enoch Pratt Free Library of Baltimore City," with power, and are required to fill any vacancies in said Board occurring by resignation, disability or otherwise, and to perpetuate their succession, and to do all necessary things for the control and management of said Library and its branches, and to perform the duties imposed on them by this act, and to receive from said Mayor and City Council of Baltimore said sum of fifty thousand dollars per annum as aforesaid, and expend the same for the purposes of said Library in such manner as they shall think proper, and to make all necessary by-laws and regulations for the government and administration of said trust, and for the appointment of the necessary officers and agents: Provided that none but citizens of Maryland, actually residing in the City of Baltimore, shall be appointed or elected as members of said Board; and provided, further, that none of the successors of said Board, or any officer thereof, shall be appointed or removed on political or religious grounds, and said Board shall have power to remove any Trustee who shall fail for six months to attend the meetings of said Board. Said Trustees shall make an annual report to the Mayor and City Council of Baltimore of their proceedings, and of the condition of said Library and its branches, with a full account of the moneys received and expended by them.

Section 3. And be it further enacted and ordained that it shall be the duty of the Mayor and City Council of Baltimore to appoint a Visitor, who shall as often as once a year examine the books and accounts of said Trustees and make a report thereof to the Mayor and City Council of Baltimore; and said Mayor and City Council shall, in case of any abuse of their powers by said Trustees or their successors, have the right to resort to the proper courts to enforce the performance of the trust hereby imposed on them.

SECTION 4. And be it enacted that the said real estate and personal property vested in said Mayor and City Council by virtue of this act, and to become so by future purchase under the provisions thereof, and the fund and franchises of "The Enoch Pratt Free Library of Baltimore City," shall be exempt from all State and municipal taxes forever.

SECTION 5. And be it further enacted, that before the ordinance which the Mayor and City Council of Baltimore are hereby authorized and empowered to pass, for the purpose of accepting said donation and entering into said contract and agreement for the payment of said sum of fifty thousand dollars annually for the maintenance of said Library, shall take effect, the said ordinance shall be approved by a majority of the votes of the legal voters of said City, cast at the time and places to be appointed by said ordinance for submitting the same to the legal voters of said City, as required by Section 7 of Article XI of the Constitution of Maryland.

SECTION 6. And be it enacted that this act shall take effect from the date of its passage.

Approved this thirtieth day of March, 1882.

WILLIAM T. HAMILTON,
                Governor.

OTIS KEILHOLTZ,
  Speaker of the House of Delegates.

GEORGE HAWKINS WILLIAMS,
          President of the Senate.

JOINT RESOLUTIONS,

Assented to by the General Assembly of Maryland at January Session, 1882.

JOINT RESOLUTIONS in relation to the gift by Enoch Pratt, Esquire, of the City of Baltimore, of over a million dollars to the Mayor and City Council of Baltimore for the establishment of a Free Circulating Library.

Whereas, Enoch Pratt, of Baltimore, has recently tendered to the Corporation of that City the munificent gift of over a million of dollars for the establishment and perpetuation of a Free Circulating Library, under conditions whose practical wisdom commends them to universal approval; and,

Whereas, neither the value and importance of such an Institution, nor the noble and generous purposes of its founder, can be measured even by the splendid liberality of its endowment; be it therefore

Resolved, By the General Assembly of Maryland, that the name of Enoch Pratt be added to the list of those public benefactors whom the people of Maryland will hold in perpetual and grateful remembrance; and it is further

Resolved, That, in placing this acknowledgment and tribute upon the permanent records of the State, it is the desire and purpose of the General Assembly not merely to signify their appreciation of a great and disinterested public service, but especially to honor a conspicuous example of the patriotism and public spirit which give to wealth its largest dignity and lift it to its highest uses. Be it further

Resolved, That a copy of these resolutions, signed by the President of the Senate and the Speaker of the House of Delegates, be transmitted to Mr. Pratt, in further token of respect.

OTIS KEILHOLTZ,
Speaker of the House of Delegates.
GEORGE HAWKINS WILLIAMS,
President of the Senate.

SUBSEQUENT ACTION OF THE CITY COUNCIL OF BALTIMORE.

Ordinance No. 106 of 1882.

An Ordinance accepting, on the part of the Mayor and City Council of Baltimore, the lot of ground, and improvements thereon, situate on Mulberry street, in the City of Baltimore, of the estimated value of two hundred and twenty-five thousand dollars, and of the sum of eight hundred and thirty-three thousand three hundred and thirty-three dollars and thirty-three cents, from Enoch Pratt, of the City of Baltimore, and contracting and agreeing on the part of said Mayor and City Council of the City of Baltimore with said Enoch Pratt for the payment of an annuity of fifty thousand dollars, payable in equal quarterly payments, by said Mayor and City Council to the Board of Trustees of "The Enoch Pratt Free Library of Baltimore City," a corporation incorporated by the General Assembly of Maryland, and to provide for the submission of this ordinance to the legal voters of Baltimore City, as required by said act and by Section 7 of Article XI of the Constitution of Maryland.

Whereas, Enoch Pratt, of the City of Baltimore, has agreed to establish a Free Public Library in the City of Baltimore, to be known as "The Enoch Pratt Free Library of Baltimore City," and has agreed to erect upon a lot of ground on Mulberry street, owned by him, a Library Building of the estimated cost of two hundred and twenty-five thousand dollars, or thereabout, and has agreed to convey said lot and premises to the Mayor and City Council of Baltimore, and also to pay unto said Mayor and City Council the sum of eight hundred and thirty-three thousand three hundred and thirty-three dollars and thirty-three cents, provided the said Mayor and City Council will accept said conveyance and said sum of money, and agree by ordinance to grant and create an annuity, and to pay annually to a Board of Trustees, and their successors, the sum of fifty thousand dollars perpetually hereafter, forever, in equal quarterly payments, for the purchase and maintenance of said Library, with not less than four branches in different parts of the City, the said branches to be established by said Trustees within such time as can be reasonably accomplished out of said quarterly payments; the title to said Library, its branches, books, and all other property, to be vested in the Mayor and City Council of Baltimore, the control and management of said Library and property to be in said Board of Trustees.

And whereas, the General Assembly of Maryland, by an act passed at its January session, eighteen hundred and eighty-two, chapter one hundred and eighty-one, authorized and empowered the said Mayor and City Council to accept the said proposal of the said Enoch Pratt, and granted full power and authority unto the said Mayor and City Council, upon the conveyance of said lot, and the improvements aforesaid, and upon said payment of said sum of money to it, by the said Enoch Pratt, to contract and agree by ordinance, to be approved by the legal voters of said City as hereinafter provided, to pay perpetually to the Board of Trustees of "The Enoch Pratt Free Library of Baltimore City" the annual sum of fifty thousand dollars in equal quarterly payments forever.

And whereas, said "Enoch Pratt Free Library of Baltimore City" has been duly incorporated by said act of said General Assembly of Maryland, and said Enoch Pratt is desirous to make the conveyance aforesaid, and to pay unto said Mayor and City Council the said sum of eight hundred and thirty-three thousand three hundred and thirty-three dollars and thirty-three cents; therefore,

SECTION 1. Be it enacted and ordained by the Mayor and City Council of Baltimore, in pursuance of the power and authority vested in it by said act of the General Assembly of Maryland, and for the purpose of perpetually promoting and diffusing knowledge and education among the people of the City of Baltimore, that the said proposed conveyance of the said Library Building and premises, situate upon Mulberry street, as aforesaid, and the said proposed payment of eight hundred and thirty-three thousand three hundred and thirty-three dollars and thirty-three cents, be and they are hereby agreed to be accepted by said Mayor and City Council of Baltimore. And, for the purpose of carrying into effect the said proposed object, the said Mayor and City Council of Baltimore by this ordinance doth hereby contract and agree with the said Enoch Pratt, and with the said "Enoch Pratt Free Library of Baltimore City," the body corporate aforesaid, in consideration of said conveyance of said Library building and premises, and of the payment of said sum of money unto it, to grant and create an annuity of fifty thousand dollars, to be paid perpetually hereafter, forever, in equal quarterly payments, for the purposes and maintenance of said Library, said annuity to be paid unto the Board of Trustees of said body corporate and their successors forever, to be applied by them to the purposes and maintenance of said Library as established and defined in the act of incorporation thereof.

SECTION 2. And be it further enacted and ordained that, upon the conveyance by said Enoch Pratt, or his representatives, by a valid deed, of the clear, unencumbered fee-simple estate in said lot of ground, with the improvements thereon, situate on Mulberry street, in said City of Baltimore, unto the said Mayor and City Council, and upon the payment by said Enoch Pratt, or his representatives, unto said Mayor and City Council of said sum of eight hundred and thirty-three thousand three hundred and thirty-three dollars and thirty-three cents, the Mayor of the City of Baltimore at the time of the execution of said deed is hereby authorized and empowered to join in the execution of the same for and on behalf of the Mayor and City Council of Baltimore, and to contract, covenant and agree for, and on their behalf to pay perpetually thereafter, the yearly sum of fifty thousand dollars in equal quarterly payments unto the Trustees of "The Enoch Pratt Free Library of Baltimore City" and their successors forever; the said "Enoch Pratt Free Library of Baltimore City" also joining in said deed, and agreeing to appropriate said sum for its corporate purposes, and to make an annual report to the Mayor and City Council of Baltimore of the proceedings of said body corporate, and of the condition of said Library and its branches, with a full account of the moneys received and expended by said Trustees.

SECTION 3. Be it further enacted and ordained that this ordinance shall be submitted to the legal voters of the City of Baltimore for their approval or disapproval, at the election to be held on the fourth Wednesday in October, eighteen hundred and eighty-two, at which election each voter who may approve the adoption of this ordinance shall deposit a ticket or ballot in the separate box hereinafter provided for, on which ticket or ballot shall be written or printed the words, "For the ordinance of the Mayor and City Council of Baltimore creating an annuity for the establishment of 'The Enoch Pratt Free Library of

Baltimore City'; and each voter who may disapprove of this ordinance shall deposit a ballot or ticket on which shall be written or printed the words, "Against the ordinance of the Mayor and City Council of Baltimore creating an annuity for the establishment of 'The Enoch Pratt Free Library of Baltimore City.'"

SECTION 4. And be it further enacted and ordained that, immediately after the closing of the polls, the judges of election of the several precincts shall count the ballots deposited at said election, and shall make return to the Mayor and City Council of Baltimore of the number of votes cast "for the ordinance of the Mayor and City Council of Baltimore creating an annuity for the establishment of 'The Enoch Pratt Free Library of Baltimore City'" and the number of votes cast "against the ordinance of the Mayor and City Council of Baltimore creating an annuity for the establishment of 'The Enoch Pratt Free Library of Baltimore City'"; and if a majority of the votes cast at said election shall be in favor of this ordinance, the said Mayor shall certify the fact to the President of each branch of the City Council, and sections one and two of this ordinance shall take effect on and from the date of said certificate.

SECTION 5. And be it further enacted and ordained that a copy of this ordinance, and notice of the day of holding such election, shall be published in at least four of the daily newspapers of the City of Baltimore twice a week for two weeks preceding said election.

Section 6. And be it further enacted and ordained that the City Comptroller be and he is hereby authorized and directed to have suitable ballot-boxes prepared and furnished to the judges of election at the designated places of voting in the precincts of the City of Baltimore, for the reception of the tickets cast for or against this ordinance; and he is further authorized and directed to have tickets of the description mentioned above printed and placed at all the polls of the said city on the day of said election; and that the City Register be and he is hereby authorized and directed to pay the expense of the preparation of said ballot-boxes, and of the printing of said tickets, and the publication of said notice, and other expenses therewith connected, out of any money in the Treasury not otherwise appropriated.

Ordinance examined by the Committee on Enrollment and found correct.

Attested by   W. Starr Gephart,
                    D. G. Wright,
                    J. B. Wentz.

I. Parker Veazey,
    President of First Branch.
Alvin Robertson,
    President of Second Branch.

Was presented to the Mayor, June 22, 1882, and on July 15, 1882, endorsed

    Approved, WM. PINKNEY WHYTE,
              Mayor.

JOHN A. ROBB,
  Register.

NOTICE OF ELECTION.

Notice is hereby given to the legal voters of the City of Baltimore, that an election will be held in the several precincts of the City on the fourth Wednesday of October, 1882 (being the twenty-fifth day of the month), for the approval or disapproval of the following ordinance, passed by the Mayor and City Council of Baltimore—viz.:

"An ordinance accepting, on the part of the Mayor and City Council of Baltimore, the lot of ground and improvements thereon situate on Mulberry street, in the City of Baltimore, of the estimated value of two hundred and twenty-five thousand dollars and of the sum of eight hundred and thirty-three thousand three hundred and thirty-three dollars and thirty-three cents, from Enoch Pratt, of the City of Baltimore, and contracting and agreeing on the part of said Mayor and City Council of the City of Baltimore, with said Enoch Pratt, for the payment of an annuity of fifty thousand dollars, payable in equal quarterly payments by said Mayor and City Council to the Board of Trustees of 'The Enoch Pratt Free Library of Baltimore City,' a corporation incorporated by the General Assembly of Maryland, and to provide for the submission of this ordinance to the legal voters of Baltimore City, as required by said act, and by Section 7 of Article XI of the Constitution of Maryland."

The polls will be opened at 6 o'clock A. M., and closed at 6 o'clock P. M.

     JOHN F. HUNTER,
       Sheriff of Baltimore City.

   MAYOR'S OFFICE, CITY HALL,
     BALTIMORE, *November* 6, 1882.
To the President of the First Branch City Council,

 Sir:—In pursuance of the 4th Section of an ordinance accepting, on the part of the Mayor and City Council of Baltimore, the lot of ground and improvements on Mulberry street from Enoch Pratt, Esq., etc., etc., I hereby certify that I have received the returns of the judges of election of the number of votes cast for said ordinance, and the number of votes cast against it, and I further certify that a majority of the votes have been cast in favor of the ordinance.

 The returns of said vote are herewith transmitted to the First Branch of the City Council.

     Yours very respectfully,
      WM. PINKNEY WHYTE,
        Mayor.

 I hereby certify that the aforegoing is a true copy of a letter received by the First Branch City Council on November 6th, A. D. 1882.

     A. V. MILHOLLAND,
       Chief Clerk.

FURTHER PROCEEDINGS OF THE CITY COUNCIL.

April 23, 1883.

The following communication was transmitted by the Mayor to the City Council, covering a copy of an ordinance entitled "An ordinance authorizing the investment in Baltimore City stock of the money proposed to be paid by Enoch Pratt for the purpose of establishing 'The Enoch Pratt Free Library of Baltimore City,' according to the terms and provisions of Ordinance No. 106, approved July 15, 1882," which was read and referred to the Joint Standing Committee on Ways and Means.

Mayor's Office, City Hall,
Baltimore, *April* 23, 1883.

To the Honorable the Members of the
First and Second Branches of the City Council,
Gentlemen :

I have been led to believe that during the summer, while the City Council may be in recess, Enoch Pratt, Esq., will be ready to convey to the Mayor and City Council the lot and improvements on Mulberry street known as "The Enoch Pratt Free Library," and also to pay to the City the sum of eight hundred and thirty-three thousand three hundred and thirty-three dollars and thirty-three cents ($833,333.33), in accordance with the terms of Ordinance No. 106, approved July 15, 1882.

In view of the obligation of the City under that ordinance to pay to the Trustees of the Library the annuity of fifty thousand dollars in quarterly payments, it is highly desirable that the large sum proposed to be paid by Mr. Pratt shall be made to bear interest as soon after its payment as practicable, so as to provide for the extinguishment, at the earliest possible day, of this annual charge; and inasmuch as authority already exists, by ordinances heretofore passed, to issue for various corporate purposes new city stock to an amount approaching one million dollars, it seems to me that it will be best to invest the money to be paid by Mr. Pratt in these new loans at par, for the purpose of a special sinking fund. Such an investment, at four per cent., will yield the annual sum of thirty-three thousand three hundred and thirty-three dollars and thirty-two cents, and by the investment of the interest also from time to time, as it matures, there will be realized in a few years an annual income equal to the annuity of fifty thousand dollars which the City has engaged to pay to the Trustees of the Library. When this point is reached, there will no longer be any occasion to continue the raising of the annuity by taxation, and the tax levied for this purpose can then be discontinued.

It is true that this plan contemplates the levy of a tax to realize annually the sum of fifty thousand dollars for the near future, and then an abandonment of that tax when the fund itself will earn a sum equal to the annuity. It may be suggested by others that the fund paid by Mr. Pratt should be invested to realize the thirty-three thousand three hundred and thirty-three dollars and thirty-two cents annually, and that the remaining sum of sixteen thousand six hundred and sixty-six dollars and sixty-eight cents should be levied perpetually as a tax, but I cannot believe this will be as satisfactory to the people as the plan I have here proposed.

In order to carry out the views here presented, I submit to you herewith the draft of an ordinance prepared at my request by the City Counsellor, which I respectfully recommend to you for passage before your adjournment for the summer recess.

    I am very respectfully,
      Your obedient servant,
        WM. PINKNEY WHYTE,
           Mayor.

Mr. Ford, from the Joint Standing Committee on Ways and Means, submitted the following report and accompanying ordinance, which was read:

The Joint Standing Committee on Ways and Means, to whom was referred an ordinance relating to " The Enoch Pratt Free Library" fund, having given the subject the consideration it deserves, beg leave to report favorably thereon, and ask the passage of the following ordinance.

JOHN T. FORD,
EDWD. LANDSTREET,
JOHN J. MAHON,
First Branch.
D. G. WRIGHT,
H. G. FLEDDERMAN,
Second Branch.

ORDINANCE NO. 64, APPROVED MAY 14, 1883.

AN ORDINANCE authorizing the investment in Baltimore City stock of the money proposed to be paid by Enoch Pratt for the purpose of establishing "The Enoch Pratt Free Library of Baltimore City," according to the terms and provisions of Ordinance No. 106, approved July 15, 1882.

SECTION 1. Be it enacted and ordained by the Mayor and City Council of Baltimore that, so soon as Enoch Pratt shall pay to the Mayor and City Council of Baltimore the sum of eight hundred and thirty-three thousand three hundred and thirty-three dollars and thirty-three cents, according to the terms and provisions of Ordinance No. 106, approved July 15th, 1882, it shall be the duty of the Commissioners of Finance to invest the same in Baltimore City stock heretofore authorized to be issued at par, as a sinking fund to be known by the name of "The Enoch Pratt Free Library Sinking Fund."

SECTION 2. And be it further enacted and ordained that the interest upon said investment so as aforesaid directed to be made shall also be invested from time to time, as the same shall be received, in the public debt of the City of Baltimore, and such investments of said interest, and of the interest upon said interest, shall also constitute a part of said sinking fund, and that said investment of said interest, and of interest on said interest, shall continue so to be made in the public debt of the City of Baltimore until the annual income from said investments shall reach the sum of fifty thousand dollars; and in the meanwhile the sum of fifty thousand dollars, to pay said annuity, shall be levied for as other City taxes are levied for.

SECTION 3. And be it further enacted and ordained that, when the said annual income upon the investments in said sinking fund shall reach the sum of fifty thousand dollars, the making of said investments for said purpose shall cease, and the said annual income of fifty thousand dollars arising therefrom shall be thereafter appropriated and applied to the payment of the annuity of fifty thousand dollars to the Trustees of "The Enoch Pratt Free Library of Baltimore City," and all taxation for the purpose of raising said annuity of fifty thousand dollars for such purpose shall cease and be discontinued.

On motion of Mr. Ford, the ordinance was read a second time, by special order, the title approved, and the same declared passed.

This ordinance was also passed by the Second Branch, April 24, and approved by the Mayor, May 14, 1883.

DEED FROM ENOCH PRATT AND WIFE TO THE MAYOR AND CITY COUNCIL OF BALTIMORE.

THIS INDENTURE, made this second (2d) day of July (A. D. 1883), eighteen hundred and eighty-three, between Enoch Pratt, of the City of Baltimore and State of Maryland, and Maria Louisa Pratt, his wife, of the first part, "The Enoch Pratt Free Library of Baltimore City" (a corporation duly incorporated by act of the General Assembly of Maryland, as hereinafter mentioned) of the second part, and the Mayor and City Council of Baltimore, a body politic and corporate, of the third part:

Witnesseth, That whereas, by an act of the General Assembly of Maryland passed at the January session, eighteen hundred and eighty-two (1882), chapter one hundred and eighty-one (181), entitled "An act to enable the Mayor and City Council of Baltimore to accept a donation from Enoch Pratt for the establishment and perpetual endowment of a Free Public Library in said City, to be known as 'The Enoch Pratt Free Library of Baltimore City,' and to provide for the appointment and incorporation of Trustees for the management thereof," the Mayor and City Council of Baltimore were authorized and empowered to accept the proposal of said Enoch Pratt as set forth in the preamble to said act.

And whereas, by said act, full power and authority were given to said Mayor and City Council of Baltimore, upon the conveyance of the lot of ground on Mulberry street, in Baltimore City, and the improvements thereon, then about to be erected by said Enoch Pratt, and upon the payment to said Mayor and City Council by said Enoch Pratt of the sum of eight hundred and thirty-three thousand three hundred and thirty-three dollars and thirty-three cents, to contract and agree by ordinance, to be approved by the legal voters of said City, to pay perpetually and forever to the Board of Trustees of "The Enoch Pratt Free Library of Baltimore City" the sum of fifty thousand dollars ($50,000) per annum in equal quarterly payments.

And whereas, in and by said act of Assembly, "The Enoch Pratt Free Library of Baltimore City" was duly created a body politic and corporate.

And whereas, by an ordinance of said Mayor and City Council passed on the first day of May (1882), eighteen hundred and eighty-two, in pursuance of the power and authority by said act of Assembly conferred on said Mayor and City Council, it was enacted and ordained that the said proposed conveyance of the said Library building and premises, situate on Mulberry street as aforesaid, and the said proposed payment of ($833,333.33) eight hundred and thirty-three thousand three hundred and thirty-three dollars and thirty-three cents, be and they were thereby agreed to be accepted, and said Mayor and City Council did thereby contract and agree with the said Enoch Pratt and with the said "Enoch Pratt Free Library of Baltimore City," a body corporate as aforesaid, in consideration of said conveyance of said Library building and premises, and of the payment of said sum of money unto it, to grant and create an annuity of fifty thousand ($50,000) dollars, to be paid perpetually thereafter forever, in equal quarterly payments, for the purposes and maintenance of said Library; said annuity to be paid unto the Board of Trustees of said body corporate and their successors forever, to be applied by them to the purposes and maintenance of said Library as established and defined by and in the Act of Incorporation thereof.

And whereas, it was in said ordinance further enacted and ordained that upon the conveyance by said Enoch Pratt, by a valid deed, of the clear, unencumbered fee-simple estate in said lot of ground, with the improvements thereon, unto the said Mayor and City Council, and upon payment by said Enoch Pratt unto said Mayor and City Council of said sum of ($833,333.33) eight hundred and thirty-three thousand three hundred and thirty-three dollars and thirty-three cents, the Mayor of the City of Baltimore at the time of the execution of the deed was thereby authorized and empowered to join in the execution of the same for and on behalf of the Mayor and City Council of Baltimore, and to contract, covenant and agree for and on their behalf to pay perpetually thereafter the yearly sum of fifty thousand ($50,000) dollars, in equal quarterly payments, unto the Trustees of "The Enoch Pratt Free Library of Baltimore City," and their successors, forever; the said "Enoch Pratt Free Library of Baltimore City" also joining in said deed, and agreeing to appropriate said sum for its corporate purposes, and to make an annual report to the Mayor and City Council of Baltimore of the proceedings of said body corporate, and of the condition of said Library and its branches, with a full account of the moneys received and expended by said Trustees.

And whereas, as was further directed by said act of Assembly and said ordinance, the same was submitted to the legal voters of Baltimore City, for approval or disapproval, at the election held on the fourth Wednesday in October in the year (1882) eighteen hundred and eighty-two, and the said ordinance at said election was, by said legal voters, duly approved.

And whereas, the said Enoch Pratt has completed the Library building on said lot of ground (the same with its improvements being valued at the sum of two hundred and fifty thousand dollars), and at and before the execution of this deed has paid to the Mayor and City Council of Baltimore the said sum of eight hundred and thirty-three thousand three hundred and thirty-three dollars and thirty-three cents the receipt of which is hereby acknowledged, making an aggregate amount in money and property so received from said Enoch Pratt of ($1,083,333.33) one million and eighty-three thousand three hundred and thirty-three dollars and thirty-three cents.

Now, therefore, this indenture witnesseth that, for and in consideration of the premises, and of the sum of five dollars paid by the said Mayor and City Council of Baltimore to the said Enoch Pratt and Maria Louisa Pratt, his wife, the receipt of which is hereby acknowledged, they, the said Enoch Pratt and Maria Louisa Pratt, his wife, do hereby grant and convey unto the Mayor and City Council of Baltimore, its successors and assigns, all that lot or parcel of ground situate in said City of Baltimore which, in the deed thereof from Charles Morton Stewart and Charles Oliver O'Donnell, trustees, etc., to said Enoch Pratt bearing date on the twentieth day of August, A. D. (1872) eighteen hundred and seventy-two, and recorded among the land records of said City in Liber G. R., No 577, folio 466, etc., is thus described, to wit: Beginning for the same on the line of the north side of Mulberry street, at the distance of one hundred and thirty feet and eleven inches easterly from the northeast corner or intersection of Mulberry and Park streets, and then running thence easterly, bounding on Mulberry street eighty feet and seven inches more or less, to a point distant one hundred and eight feet west from the west side of Cathedral street, thence northerly parallel to Park street one hundred and forty feet, to an alley twenty feet wide, called N Alley, thence westerly, bounding on south side of N Alley eighty feet and seven inches more or less, to intersect a line drawn from the place of beginning northerly, parallel to Park street, and thence southerly, reversing the line so drawn one hundred and forty feet to the place of beginning.

Together with the buildings and improvements thereon, and the rights, privileges, easements, advantages and appurtenances thereunto belonging or appertaining.

To have and to hold the property, lot of ground and premises above-described, with the buildings and improvements thereon, and all the rights, privileges, easements, advantages and appurtenances thereunto belonging or in anywise appertaining as aforesaid, unto the Mayor and City Council of Baltimore, its successors and assigns, in fee-simple forever; in trust, nevertheless, for the uses and purposes herein mentioned and set forth.

And said Enoch Pratt doth hereby covenant that he will warrant specially the property hereby conveyed, and that he will execute such further assurances as may be requisite for the confirmation of these presents.

And this indenture further witnesseth that, for and in consideration of the premises, and of the said sum of money by said Enoch Pratt paid and transferred to the said Mayor and City Council of Baltimore, and in consideration of this conveyance, the Mayor and City Council of Baltimore aforesaid, for and on its own behalf, and for its successors, doth hereby contract, covenant and agree with the said "Enoch Pratt Free Library of Baltimore City," and its successors, to pay yearly and every year forever to "The Enoch Pratt Free Library of Baltimore City," and its Trustees and their successors, the sum of fifty thousand ($50,000) dollars, in equal quarterly instalments, accounting from the first day of July, A. D. (1883) eighteen hundred and eighty-three.

And this indenture further witnesseth that, for and in consideration of the premises and of the payment of the said annual sum agreed to be paid as aforesaid, "The Enoch Pratt Free Library of Baltimore City," for itself and its successors, doth hereby covenant, contract and agree with said Mayor and City Council of Baltimore, and its successors, to appropriate any and all of the annual sums by it to be received entirely and solely for its corporate purposes; and, further, that the said "Enoch Pratt Free Library of Baltimore City" will make annual reports to the Mayor and City Council of Baltimore of the proceedings of the said body corporate, and of the condition of said Library and its branches, with a full account of the moneys received and expended by said Trustees.

And it is further hereby provided that the Mayor and City Council of Baltimore and "The Enoch Pratt Free Library of Baltimore City" may by joint deed sell and convey the real estate herein conveyed, or any real or leasehold estate which may hereafter be vested in the said Mayor and City Council of Baltimore for the purposes of the trust by this deed created, and the proceeds of sale shall be paid to said "Enoch Pratt Free Library of Baltimore City," to be invested by it, with the approval of said Mayor and City Council, in other property for the purposes of this trust.

And this indenture further witnesseth that the Mayor and City Council of Baltimore doth hereby constitute and appoint Samuel Turner Duvall to be its attorney for it and in its name, and as its act and deed to acknowledge this indenture, to the intent that the same may be duly recorded. And "The Enoch Pratt Free Library of Baltimore City" doth hereby constitute and appoint Stewart Brown to be its attorney for it and in its name, and as its act and deed to acknowledge this indenture, to the intent that the same may be duly recorded.

In witness whereof, the said Enoch Pratt and Maria Louisa Pratt, his wife, the parties of the first part hereto, have hereunto subscribed their names and affixed their seals on the day and year first herein written; and William Pinkney Whyte, Mayor of Baltimore City, has hereunto subscribed his name and caused the corporate seal of the Mayor and City Council of Baltimore to be hereunto affixed; and Enoch Pratt, the President of "The Enoch Pratt Free Library of Baltimore City," has hereunto subscribed his name and caused the corporate seal of said corporation to be hereto affixed on said day and year.

Signed, sealed and delivered in the presence of Joshua M. Myers, John A. Robb, witnesses as to the signatures of W. P. Whyte, *Mayor*, and Enoch Pratt, *President*.

     ENOCH PRATT.   [Seal.]
     MARIA LOUISA PRATT. [Seal.]
     WM. PINKNEY WHYTE, *Mayor*.

ENOCH PRATT,
 Pres't Enoch Pratt Free Library of Baltimore.

STATE OF MARYLAND, CITY OF BALTIMORE, to wit:

I hereby certify that on this second day of July, A. D. (1883) eighteen hundred and eighty-three, before me, the subscriber, a Justice of the Peace of said State, in and for said City, personally appeared Enoch Pratt and Maria Louisa Pratt, his wife, and acknowledged the foregoing deed to be their respective act and deed; and at the same time also appeared Samuel Turner Duvall, an attorney of the Mayor and

City Council of Baltimore, constituted by a power of attorney in the within deed, and acknowledged the within deed to be the act and deed of the Mayor and City Council of Baltimore.

And at the same time also appeared Stewart Brown, an attorney of "The Enoch Pratt Free Library of Baltimore City," constituted by a power of attorney in the within deed, and acknowledged the said deed to be the act and deed of "The Enoch Pratt Free Library of Baltimore City."

JOSHUA M. MYERS, *J. P.*

Title and deed approved June 29th, 1883.

JOHN GILL, JR.,
Examiner of Titles.

FURTHER ACTION OF THE CITY COUNCIL ACCEPTING THE DEED OF PROPERTY FROM ENOCH PRATT AND WIFE.

Whereas, in pursuance of Ordinance No. 106, approved July 15th, 1882, entitled "An ordinance accepting, on the part of the Mayor and City Council of Baltimore, the lot of ground and improvements thereon situate on Mulberry street, in the City of Baltimore, of the estimated value of two hundred and twenty-five thousand dollars, and of the sum of $833,333.33, from Enoch Pratt, of the City of Baltimore, and contracting and agreeing on the part of the said Mayor and City Council with said Enoch Pratt for the payment of an annuity of fifty thousand dollars, payable in equal quarterly payments, by the said Mayor and City Council, to the Board of Trustees of 'The Enoch Pratt Free Library of Baltimore City'"; the terms and conditions of the ordinance aforesaid having been complied with by Enoch Pratt; and

Whereas, under a condition of the contract in the foregoing connection, the Mayor and City Council of Baltimore was, on the 1st of October instant, indebted to "The Enoch Pratt Free Library of Baltimore City" the sum of twelve thousand five hundred dollars, as the quarterly payment then due, and for which no provision for the payment has been made by the

Mayor and City Council of Baltimore, because the contract aforesaid was not consummated at the time the general appropriation bill was pending in the City Council; therefore,

Resolved, by the Mayor and City Council of Baltimore, that the sum of twelve thousand five hundred dollars be and the same is hereby appropriated to pay the quarter-yearly instalment on said annuity of the said Mayor and City Council of Baltimore, due on the 1st day of October, 1883; and the Comptroller of the City be and he is hereby authorized and directed to issue his warrant on the City Register of Baltimore to pay to Enoch Pratt, the President of "The Enoch Pratt Free Library of Baltimore City," the amount aforesaid, to be taken out of any money that may be in the City treasury.

Examined by the Committee on Enrolment and found correct.

    Attested by
        DANIEL G. WRIGHT,
        JOHN J. MAHON,
        HENRY N. BANKARD.

JAMES W. DENNY, *President of 1st Branch.*
ALVIN ROBERTSON, *President of 2d Branch.*

Was presented to the Mayor October 10, 1883, and on same day endorsed,
 Approved.   WM. PINKNEY WHYTE,
              Mayor.

LETTER OF ENOCH PRATT, FORMALLY TRANSFERRING THE MANAGEMENT OF THE LIBRARY TO THE BOARD OF TRUSTEES.

BALTIMORE, *October* 1, 1884.

TO THE BOARD OF TRUSTEES OF

"THE ENOCH PRATT FREE LIBRARY OF BALTIMORE CITY."

Messrs. Enoch Pratt, George Wm. Brown, Nathaniel H. Morison, Henry Janes, Charles J. Bonaparte, George B. Cole, Edward Stabler, Jr., James A. Gary, John W. McCoy.

Gentlemen: I have the pleasure to inform you that, after over three years of constant labor and supervision, the Library buildings are completed.

The main building, on Mulberry street, is fireproof, and the four branches are located corner Fremont and Pitcher streets, corner Hollins and Calhoun streets, corner Light and Gittings streets, and corner O'Donnell and Canton streets.

These, I think, are all accessible to the people, who, I hope, will avail of the advantages it is my wish to offer them, they being for all, rich and poor, without distinction of race or color, who, when properly accredited, can take out the books, if they will handle them carefully and return them.

In each building there is an ample reading-room,

which I expect will be used in addition to the distribution of books.

I now hand the management over to you, not doubting you will make all proper arrangements to carry out my wishes and make the Institution what I wish for the people of Baltimore and State of Maryland.

I leave it to you with confidence. In my opinion, much depends on the selection of a Librarian and organizing a proper system. I would suggest your availing of the experience of old, well-established circulating libraries, and proceed with caution.

I hope the Library has a long future, and I want it to commence right.

In my letter to the Mayor and City Council of Baltimore, January 21st, 1882, I agreed to pay for the annuity of $50,000, payable quarterly, when the building on Mulberry street was completed. Wishing to have my plans fully carried out in my lifetime, I paid for the annuity on 1st July, 1883, fifteen months in advance of its completion.

I have used the quarterly payments in building the branches.

THE ACCOUNT NOW STANDS:

Paid for ground and building, Mulberry street	$250,000.00
Paid the City of Baltimore	833,333.33
Paid for the four branches	50,000.00
Cash on hand	12,500.00
Making the sum total of	$1,145,833.33

(one million one hundred and forty-five thousand eight hundred and thirty-three dollars and thirty-three cents) as the actual sum I have paid the City for the $50,000 annuity, or about $4\frac{1}{3}$ per cent. interest.

I wish to return my thanks to the architect, Charles L. Carson, and the contractors, S. H. & J. F. Adams, and all the sub-contractors and laborers who have been connected with the erection of the buildings, for their faithful services, and especially to the gentlemen who have given so much of their time and talents in assisting me in the plans and arrangements.

Now, if spared to see the Library in full and successful working order and appreciated by my fellow-citizens, I shall pass to a future life with the self-consciousness that I have contributed my mite for the talent entrusted to me.

ENOCH PRATT.

THE FORMAL OPENING OF THE LIBRARY,

ACADEMY OF MUSIC,

Monday, January 4, 1886, at 12 o'clock M.

Addresses Delivered upon the Occasion, etc.

PROGRAMME.

Prayer . . . . . Rev. Chas. R. Weld, B. D.
Address . Hon. James Hodges, Mayor, Chairman.
Address . . . . Enoch Pratt, Esq.
Address . . . Hon. Henry Lloyd, Governor.*
Oration . . . . . Hon. Geo. Wm. Brown.
Address . . . . . Hon. J. Morrison Harris.
Address . . . . . . Hon. F. C. Latrobe.
Address . . . . Dr. L. H. Steiner, Librarian.

* Governor Lloyd was prevented by Executive business from being present.

PRAYER.

In the presence of a large and appreciative audience, presided over by the Hon. James Hodges, Mayor of the City, the dedication ceremonies were opened by the following prayer by the Rev. Charles R. Weld, B. D., Minister of the First Independent Church of Baltimore:

Infinite and Holy! Giver of every good and perfect gift! We bow in reverence before the majesty of Thy sacred presence. We invoke Thy divine blessing upon the purpose of this hour. We would dedicate yonder building to Thy glory and to the free uses of the inhabitants of this City. We pray that it may be the home of a literature, pure, sound, wholesome, inspiring; that it may be a fountain from whence the mighty thoughts of the undying dead and the deathless living shall flow, in higher hopes, in purer purposes, in loftier incentives, in holier ambitions, to enrich the life of this great age and hasten the coming of Thy Kingdom on earth among men. Fill his heart with gratitude whom Thou hast permitted to see the glory of this day—to witness the completed and crowned end of his efforts. May this hour be to him like fruit from the tree of life! Bless, we pray Thee, those to whom is entrusted the burden of honor and responsibility in the development of the lasting interests of this Institution. Bless, we pray Thee, the President of these United States, the Governor of this Commonwealth, the official head of this great City. And now to Thy superintending providence we commit the future of this Institution—the issues of this hour—in the name of Him, our Lord, who has taught us to pray, Our Father, who art in heaven, hallowed be Thy name. Thy kingdom come. Thy will be done on earth, as it is in heaven. Give us this day our daily bread. And forgive us our trespasses, as we forgive those who trespass against us. And lead us not into temptation; but deliver us from evil. For Thine is the kingdom, and the power, and the glory, for ever and ever. Amen and Amen.

ADDRESS OF HON. JAMES HODGES, MAYOR.

LADIES AND GENTLEMEN:

It is known that Mr. Enoch Pratt in 1882 offered to establish an Institution in this community, to be known as "The Enoch Pratt Free Library of Baltimore City," upon certain conditions, and that the Mayor and City Council of Baltimore, being authorized and empowered by the Legislature of Maryland to do so, accepted his proposal. Mr. Pratt agreed to erect upon a lot of ground on Mulberry street, owned by him, a Library building of the estimated cost of two hundred and twenty-five thousand dollars ($225,000), and to convey said lot and premises to the Mayor and City Council of Baltimore; and, also, to pay unto said Mayor and City Council the sum of eight hundred and thirty-three thousand three hundred and thirty-three dollars and thirty-three cents, ($833,333.33); provided the said Mayor and City Council would accept said conveyance and said sum of money, and agree by Ordinance to grant and create an annuity, and to pay annually to a Board of Trustees, and their successors, the sum of fifty thousand dollars ($50,000), perpetually thereafter, forever, in quarterly payments, for the purchase and maintenance of said Library, with not less than four branches in different parts of the city, the said branches to be established by the Trustees within such time as their construction could be reasonably accomplished out of said quarterly payments; the title to said Library, its branches, books, and all other property, to be vested in the Mayor and City Council of Baltimore.

For the annuity of fifty thousand dollars ($50,000) (being about four and one-third per cent. interest on the amount invested,) which the City agreed to pay to the Trustees of "The Enoch Pratt Free Library," the sum of One million one hundred and forty-five thousand eight hundred and thirty-three dollars and thirty-three cents ($1,145,833.33) has been contributed by Mr. Pratt for the Library and its uses, made up of the following items:

Paid for ground and building, Mulberry street	$250,000.00
Paid the City of Baltimore	833,333.33
Paid for the four branches	50,000.00
Cash on hand	12,500.00
	$1,145,833.33

In further elucidation of the financial condition of the Enoch Pratt Free Library Fund, it may be said that the money contributed in July, 1883, by Mr. Pratt, toward the endowment of the Institution, has been invested by the Commissioners of Finance in the bonded debt of the City, and that the original amount, with the increment, has raised the value of the

Enoch Pratt Sinking Fund to Nine hundred and one thousand eight hundred dollars ($901,800), represented by Seven hundred and fifty-seven thousand three hundred dollars ($757,300) four per cent. stock, Ninety-five thousand three hundred dollars ($95,300) five per cent. stock, and Forty-nine thousand two hundred dollars ($49,200) six per cent. stock, yielding an annual interest of Thirty-eight thousand dollars ($38,000), being only Twelve thousand dollars ($12,000) per annum less than the amount required for the support of the Library. It is estimated that the accretion of interest during the ensuing five years, added to the principal sum, will make The Enoch Pratt Free Library self-sustaining.

Ladies and gentlemen: Now, we have assembled to-day to inaugurate, with appropriate ceremonies, the Library thus established, and for which such ample provision has been made. It is a notable event in the history of Baltimore, and marks an epoch in its progress. And as, at such epochs in the life of an individual or of a community, it is good to cast a glance backward and note the distance traversed, so here we are tempted to look back for a moment to the past of the English-speaking race, and to link the event we now celebrate, with one beneficent in its purpose, far-reaching in its consequences, which shines like a star in the twilight of English history.

Just a thousand years ago, to a year, the greatest

king that ever sat on the English throne, having delivered his people from invasion and oppression, cast about to see what was the next best service he could do them—what next royal gift should follow liberty and peace? His answer to this question was remarkable for a king of the ninth century. He determined to give them books.

So he set scribes to work to make copies of the few good books that could be found, and he himself found time to translate from the Latin into his mother tongue — literally the "King's English" — three books which seemed to him, next to the Holy Scriptures, the best that he knew of upon earth. One of these was a book of history, one a book of philosophy, and one a book of religion: the story of life in the past, counsel for life in the present, and guidance toward life in the future. Though but three, so comprehensive was their scope, so near did they come to occupying the whole domain of serious human thought, that I think I am justified in saying that in these three Alfred founded a library.

Where did he place these books? In the ninth century there was but one place that was free to all alike—as free to the serf as to the lord, to the peasant as to the king, and this was the church. So he placed these books in the churches, where all that could, might read them. But these precious volumes, laboriously penned on parchment by the long toil of patient scribes, could not be lightly risked from their appointed custody, and those who wished to read them had to read them in their place. And yet so generous was the King, so thoughtful of the needs of scholars, and so anxious that his bounty might bear full fruit, that he allowed even these books, under certain conditions, to be borrowed. So we may say that one thousand years ago, the first English free lending library was founded, as to-day we inaugurate the newest. And, as in the days of Alfred, a man among us having the ability and the will to bestow a princely gift upon his fellow-men, who already possess the blessings of liberty and peace, elects to give them books.

I might here ask you to give a glance down these thousand years, and mark what they have brought; to note the broadening and deepening of the stream of literature; the invention of printing, which placed what before was the costly luxury of the few within reach of all—making all mankind co-heirs of the great heritage of human thought, spreading knowledge abroad like the universal sunshine, which brightens alike the cottage and the palace, so that the newsboy, the bootblack, may, if he will, share treasures once beyond the reach of kings.

We pride ourselves, and not without justice, on our public schools. We have determined that no member of the community, so far as we can prevent it, shall be debarred from his share of the common heritage, and we make the opportunities of education as broad as a generous public-school system could effect it.

But, in doing this, we but place the key of knowledge into the student's hand. It is another task to fill the treasury into which that key opens. Thus the public library is the complement of the public school, and carries on the work which that has begun. For education is not an absolute, but a relative good; all depends upon the use that is made of it. If it makes a man more potent for good, it also makes him more potent for evil. It is like a sword with which a man can defend his home, but with which, also, he can slay his friend. If you look at the criminal annals, you will find that the most malignant, treacherous and far-reaching crimes, black conspiracies, gigantic frauds, secret subtle murders, have been the work of what are called educated men. But this is not an argument against education: it only reminds us that education is not sufficient in itself to make good citizens. When we have equipped the youth with fluent knowledge of several languages, have made him a skillful penman and accountant, have given him some insight into chemistry, physics and biology, we have but placed him at the parting of the ways; he may pervert all the knowledge we have given him to an instrument of evil. This we cannot prevent. But what we can do is this: we can come before the young minds, ready and eager for knowledge, and offer them such knowledge as will make them better citizens and better men. At that critical period, when good and evil influences are contending in the soul of the youth, when temptations are the strongest, and the power of resistance weakest, we can place all the incitements, all the allurements, all the opportunities, on the side of the good. Is he ambitious? We offer him the lives of the men whose deeds have won them true glory, and whom mankind delights to honor. Does his fancy turn to war and martial exploits? We place in his hands the story of the gallant struggle of the Dutch for liberty, or the heroic career of the noble-hearted Gordon. Is his imagination inflamed with wild adventure? He can follow Greeley on his mission of mercy to Arctic seas, and Polar desolations, or plunge, with Stanley, into the mysterious heart of burning Africa. In a word, there is no taste, except the absolutely vicious, which a library cannot provide for, and give a leaning toward the good.

Not the modern scholar merely, but the man of business, the merchant, the mechanic, touches the world of thought at a thousand points. To understand even the morning's paper, presupposes at least *some* knowledge of half the circle of the sciences.

Books in private or public collections are a necessity of life. By them we are able to place what we think and do, in relation with what mankind is thinking and doing. We touch the great electric chain that links together the human race, the past as well as the present. Nay, in a librarian sense there is no past for us, and the great men of old still live. The great writers of all ages are still alive for us. We can choose our companions among the wisest, best, noblest and most charming of men, and a library is a reception-room where these men will meet us and talk to us by the hour.

Though I will not say that a zeal for learning has ever eaten up the people of Baltimore, or that we have aspired to the distinction of "the Athens of America," yet we have never wanted those who loved, and who helped forward liberal studies and tastes. The noble library that we open to-day is the successor of a line of libraries founded or assisted by private liberality. Of these another may speak.

Truly Baltimore has had reason to be proud of her citizens; of some who are still with us, and of some who have departed; men, who, like Peabody, Hopkins, Moses Sheppard, Thomas Wilson and others, have recognized that they were but stewards of the wealth with which Providence had blessed them, and held it in trust for uses of good. Such a citizen is he who has founded this noble Institution, and, as with George Peabody and Johns Hopkins, and Sheppard and Wilson, Baltimore is the City of his adoption, not of his nativity.

I have known that citizen for forty years, and few, outside of his daily associates, have had a better opportunity of learning his characteristics. For nearly three years we served together on the Board of Commissioners of Finance of this City, and there I saw exemplified those traits of character which have given Enoch Pratt so eminent a reputation as a merchant and financier. He combines, to an extraordinary degree, breadth and penetration of intellectual vision; his comprehension of financial propositions is almost instantaneous, and as prompt and sure is his power to winnow the grain from the chaff, and note an unsound spot in a plausible scheme.

As a merchant, respected for his wisdom, honored for his integrity, he has lived among us for the greater part of a long life. At once energetic and unobtrusive, he has never sought posts of honor, nor ever shirked posts of duty. His hand has been felt for good in public affairs, when few knew the guiding spirit; and his quiet voice has given wise counsel and asked no meed of praise.

With him, temperament and judgment are so evenly balanced that his determination is almost intuitive, and rarely needs reconsideration. His confidence is not lightly given, nor, when given, is it lightly shaken. It is a plant of slow growth, but it strikes its roots deep and strong.

Mr. Pratt's fortune was not won by speculation; it

is not the unwilling tribute paid by rashness or folly, to shrewdness or craft. It has been the steady accumulation of a life devoted to legitimate business. He saw his purposes clearly before him, as the mariner sees his guiding star, and he never deviated from his course, until his voyage was successfully accomplished. Nor did he seek fortune for the mere sake of accumulation, and to be pointed out as a rich man. In that respect he somewhat resembles the elder Vanderbilt, of whom it was said that, in his early life at least, he did not care for money, but he *did* care to carry his point.

Few have surpassed him in the power of close and minute investigation into details, and nothing relative to any plan under his consideration, escapes his observation, or is denied its due weight. In the choice of co-operators, and in the direction of their activity, he has shown that high administrative power which, in the fields of Commerce and Finance, as in other fields, marks the leader of men.

Of Mr. Pratt's many public and private charities I shall not speak; but I cannot forbear to mention one act that shows the benevolence of his heart. Some years ago he sold a farm in Virginia to a worthy but poor young man for $20,000. The purchaser had paid, from time to time, one-half the purchase money, when a series of bad seasons and failure of crops made it impossible for him to meet the subsequent payments. Mr. Pratt sent for him, and learned the facts. After expressing sympathy for the young man's misfortunes, and encouraging him to persevere and hope, he cancelled his note for the balance due— ten thousand dollars—and handed him a valid deed for the property. Astonished and overwhelmed by this princely liberality, the recipient uttered a few broken words and retired from his benefactor's presence. Not until he had reached his Virginia home was he able to find words to express his gratitude.

The instruction of the people has always been near to the heart of Mr. Pratt. The foundation of this library is a natural sequence to the Pratt Free School, which he founded in 1865 in Middleborough, Massachusetts, which is still in successful operation. From that time to this he has revolved plans for educational advancement.

Desirous of bestowing some worthy gift upon his fellow-citizens of Baltimore, he concluded that one of the greatest needs of the City was a free public library. The Peabody Library is a grand foundation, worthy of the generous man to whom it owes its existence, and its stores are of inestimable value; but it is of a different character, and meets other wants. Mr. Pratt's design was to found a library of good reading for the entire public, of books which might be read at the fireside, and should carry their stores of knowledge, of beauty, or of innocent recreation, to the homes of the people. The plan, as the founder matured it, and as it will be explained to you in detail, consists of a central collection, worthily—indeed magnificently—housed, with branches in several sections of the city, each branch to be a minor but representative library, and all in communication with the Central Library and its ample stores.

I have spoken of the past and of the present; let me cast one single glance into the future.

Who can estimate the results, in the years to come, of the Institution we inaugurate to-day? The benefits of a library are not of the kind that force themselves upon the imagination. So, too, are the beneficent operations of Nature. The bursting torrent may inundate a valley, the cyclone may turn a smiling land into ruin and devastation; but it is the soft pervasiveness of the summer rain that quickens the parched fields into verdure, and makes the whole horizon laugh with the glad promise of the golden harvest.

It is *in* this constant, silent, and pervasive influence of the library that its power resides. Who can conjecture how many homes it will brighten?—how many firesides will be made more attractive than the saloon or the gaming-house?—how often it will place the golden key of knowledge in the hand of struggling talent; how often it may kindle the first sparks of unrecognized genius?—to how many will it bring help and solace in the conflict of daily life? to how many it will open new horizons and unknown skies?

When years shall have passed away; when the founder and we his contemporaries have departed; when this City has doubled its population, and this Library, always growing, offers to the Baltimore of another century the works of authors now unborn; when Science shall have realized some of its proudest hopes, and answers have been found to some of the enigmas which now perplex mankind; while all the time this Institution has been faithful to its duty of disseminating among the people whatever is best in human thought, then let a balance-sheet be struck and an estimate of this great benefaction be made up, then let some Baltimorean of the twentieth century stand where I am standing, and, seeing clearly the past as I see dimly the future, remind his fellow-citizens what they owe to Enoch Pratt.

ADDRESS OF ENOCH PRATT.

It is with great pleasure and satisfaction I meet you to inaugurate the opening of "The Enoch Pratt Free Library of Baltimore City," which I proposed to establish in my letter to the Mayor and City Council, January 21, 1882, and after four years of labor to inform you of the completion in the most thorough and substantial manner of the fine library buildings, and the collecting of over 32,000 volumes of books arranged for your use.

I have the greater satisfaction of knowing and seeing my plans completed as I designed them.

It may be proper for me to more fully explain my meaning of a free circulating Library. It is not free for you to take the books as you please and return them or not, but is free from charge for the use of them.

To protect the Library, the Trustees have adopted rules gathered from experience in other cities, which, I have no doubt, you will find satisfactory when you become accustomed to them.

I consider the plan adopted to secure the annuity fund for the support and increase of the Library as the great feature, and about the only thing I ask credit for. As it is founded on a rock, according to Scripture, it must stand.

Now, in the hope of God's blessing, I hand it over to you, expecting you will foster, protect and increase it, that its beneficent influences may be for the benefit of the present and all future generations, as long as our beloved city of Baltimore shall exist.

My work is finished. I am satisfied.

THE ORATION BY HON. GEORGE WM. BROWN, OF THE BOARD OF TRUSTEES.

Every city, like every individual, has a distinctive character which is derived from many sources, and has also its own laws of growth and development. We have assembled to-day to celebrate an important event in the life of this City which invites us to look backward as well as forward. The people of Maryland, at an early period, seem to have entertained the expectation that in the nature of things, a large town would spring up somewhere near the headwaters of the Chesapeake, but it was only after several experiments had been made and had failed, that the proper site appeared to be the spot on which we now stand—a point about midway between the North and South of the country, and in closer proximity to the West than the other cities of the seaboard.

As a consequence of its favorable position, the little town of Baltimore, laid out in 1734 by the county surveyor on the humble scale of sixty lots in all, each containing about one acre, began, after nearly thirty years of patient waiting, to acquire a healthy and, for that period, a remarkably rapid growth. Enterprising men of business from other parts of Maryland, as well as from her sister provinces, and from England,

Ireland and Scotland, and a few from the continent of Europe, were attracted to the new and thriving settlement. In 1756 many of the French inhabitants of Acadia, or Nova Scotia, as it is now called, who had been ruthlessly expelled from their homes by the British on their occupation of that province, found shelter here, and the part of the town where they resided was long known as Frenchtown.

In 1793, during the epoch of the French Revolution, a large and valuable accession of French population from San Domingo took refuge in Baltimore, in order to escape the revolutionary outbreak in that island. From such beginnings, and from the traditional habit of the people of Maryland to welcome all comers, without regard to country, race or religion, it naturally followed that the citizens of Baltimore have always been characterized by a freedom from provincialism, by a liberal disposition to adopt new ideas and methods, and by their hospitable reception of strangers. Before the last century closed it came to pass that the white sails of her commerce were to be seen far and near in many waters, while the inland country was traversed by huge wagons, canvas-covered, drawn by two, four, and even six horses, carrying the necessaries of civilized life to distant towns and hamlets, whence they were distributed to the surrounding country up to the borders of the ever-retreating wilderness, and whence came in return the abundant products of the fertile and virgin soil.

Amid all this traffic the amenities and amusements of life were not forgotten. The first theatre built in the colonies was at Annapolis, in 1782. During the War of the Revolution dramatic exhibitions were prohibited, but soon after its close they obtained a permanent home in Baltimore. Long after this, and when I first knew them, they were of a high character. An occasional visit to the old Holliday Street Theatre to hear one of Shakespeare's plays rendered by the excellent stock company of that day was the supreme delight of my boyhood. I remember, in *Henry IV* the manager, Wood, as a right royal Prince Hal, Wm. Warren, Sr., as a veritable Falstaff—even in size—and the elder Joseph Jefferson, who in that play was only the First Carrier, remains to this day impressed on my memory as the very drollest and most charming of comedians. He could, when he pleased, with his contagious laugh behind the scenes, before he reached the stage to make his first bow, create a ripple of merriment through the expectant audience. Still later Junius Brutus Booth rendered the part of Richard III. as fascinating as it was terrible by the flashes of his genius.

But, although in the early days of Baltimore her business men were distinguished for their sagacity, spirit and enterprise, and although there were eminent names in the learned professions, and although the social graces and enjoyments were successfully cultivated, it did not necessarily follow that public libraries and other means for liberal culture would be adequately provided. On the contrary, their appearance was postponed to a much later period.

Yet efforts in that direction were not wanting. The chief of these was the establishment of the Library Company of Baltimore in 1795. It was a stock company, and, therefore, its benefits were confined to a few. It was selected with great care, and contained many valuable volumes, but, unfortunately, adequate provision was not made for a constant supply of new books, and this fatal deficiency ruined the hopeful enterprise, and soon after the establishment of the Maryland Historical Society, in 1844, this collection of books was transferred to that body, and became the foundation of its library. No public library can be long self-sustaining. It needs a generous hand both for its endowment and support. And yet the old Baltimore Library did good work while it lasted, and I feel greatly obliged to my two grandfathers, one a doctor of divinity and one a doctor of medicine, that they were among its founders, for by their means I became free of its stores. It is true that I read a good many novels and plays which perhaps I ought not to have read, and neglected to read other books which I ought to have read; but none the less am I indebted to the old library for some of the purest enjoyments, as well as the best inspirations, of my life. I have a kindly recollection, too, of its ancient librarian, the only one in the whole establishment, although I had occasional encounters with him for the last new book, particularly if it was of the amusing sort, which he sometimes, as I suspected, kept stored away for a privileged reader, if not for his own perusal.

In 1839 the Mercantile Library was founded with the object of supplying in some measure the necessity for books then felt by a number of persons. As it was supported by the annual subscription of members, its resources were necessarily limited, but, being in excellent hands, it for many years furnished an important part of the intellectual food of the people. Its usefulness still continues by the generous aid of Mr. John W. McCoy, and I am sure I express the desire which many feel that this library should always be maintained for the benefit of a large class whose wants can nowhere else be so well supplied. In 1857 George Peabody, of London, and previously of this city, established in his lifetime the Peabody Institute, a great work in itself, and still greater for the noble example thus set, the far-reaching and beneficial effects of which cannot be estimated. The Institute contains a library for reference and research which by its extent and completeness commands the admiration of all scholars, and which continues to increase so rapidly as to meet the demands of that portion of the community. There are in Baltimore various other libraries, designed mainly for the use of particular professions or classes, some large and excellent of their kind, all doubtless doing good service in supplying special wants; but all the libraries in the City, valuable as they are, indispensable as some are, fail to reach the great need of the mass of the community. This need is of modern growth. When the old Library Company to which I have referred was established in 1795, the schoolmaster and schoolmistress had not been abroad. It is not strange that a library company should at that period have been founded for the benefit chiefly of the stockholders and their families. It had not then entered into the minds of men that it is the duty of the State to instruct the whole people, and until the people are instructed they cannot be readers and have little need of books. The effect of public schools has been to create a host of readers. Without books, progress in liberal education must cease with the close of schooldays, and at a period where, instead of closing, it ought to take a new departure and lead up to the great end of all education—a higher and nobler life. Enoch Pratt was among the first to perceive this, and he took the subject into serious consideration. In large cities there are always to be found among the men who are most prominent, useful and successful in the different walks of life, those who in their youth came from smaller towns or rural districts. Mr. Pratt belongs to this number. Born in North Middleborough, Mass., and having received his commercial education in Boston, he came here at the age of twenty-three and established himself in the iron business, which he still continues. Prosperity soon followed—not rapidly, but steadily, because it was based on those qualities of honesty, industry, sagacity and energy which, mingled with thrift, although they cannot be said to insure success, are certainly most likely to achieve it. Mr. Pratt and myself have been friends for many years. After he had become a thriving merchant, and when I was a painstaking lawyer, he came to me for legal advice, and as the library question necessarily had a legal side, he frequently consulted me on the subject. In this way I came to know more than any one except Mr. Pratt himself in regard to his intention to found a free library.

Wherever civilization flourishes there must be libraries, and they must be accessible to scholars. From its very nature, a library should be diffusive in its character. It would seem from recent investigations that the library at Nineveh of the monarch Sardanapalus, 820 years before Christ, was thrown open for the general use of the king's subjects; and the inscription said to have been placed on the famous library which the Egyptian king, Rameses the First, founded in the fourteenth century before

Christ, tells its own story. That inscription was, 'The Dispensary of the Soul.'

But the idea of a free circulating library for a large city is of recent origin. It became the fixed purpose of Mr. Pratt that whatever he did must be for the benefit of the whole people of the city of his adoption. His plan gradually took its present shape, and it contains some new and valuable features, both as regards the character of its administration and the permanent provision made for its support. The Library could be established only by a large and generous gift of money.

Mr. Pratt belongs to a school of business men, now somewhat obsolete, by whom fortunes are made not by great and speculative enterprises, but by patient industry. Although a man of wealth, a million of dollars and upwards is to him a large sum of money. His riches have never grown so great as to bring down on him the infliction of any of the new-fangled titles which are used to decorate the members of our American plutocracy. He is not known even in the newspapers as a "Railroad King" or a "Merchant Prince," but simply as Enoch Pratt, sometime and now merchant and banker; and yet the time has already come when he, like George Peabody, has earned a distinction far worthier and more enduring than any title—the rare distinction of having in his lifetime devoted a large portion of his fortune to the promotion of the happiness and welfare of his fellow-citizens. Only a man of generosity and force of character as well, is capable of making such a sacrifice.

Mr. Pratt has explained his plan, and you are entitled to hear it in his own words. On the 21st of January, 1882, he addressed a letter to the Mayor and City Council of Baltimore in which he said that for some years he had contemplated establishing a free circulating library for the benefit of the whole city, and, in pursuance of this plan, the excavation of the foundation had already been commenced, and that he had entered into a contract to erect a fire-proof building on his Mulberry street lot, capable of holding two hundred thousand volumes, and that his purpose was to have branches connected with it in the four quarters of the City, under the same management. He estimated that the building would cost about $225,000, and upon its completion he proposed to convey it to the City. The title to all the books and property was also to be vested in the City, to which he agreed to pay, on the completion of the building, the additional sum of $833,333.33⅓, provided the City would grant an annuity of $50,000 per annum forever, payable quarterly to the Board of Trustees of the Library, for the support and maintenance of the Library and its branches. He proposed that a Board of nine Trustees should be incorporated for the management of the Library; that the Trustees should be selected by himself from our best citizens, and that all vacancies which should occur should be filled by the Board.

The articles of incorporation were to contain a provision that no Trustee or officer should be appointed or removed on religious or political grounds. The Trustees were to receive from the City the quarterly payments, and to expend them in their discretion for the benefit of the Library. It was believed, he added, that this annual payment would afford a sufficient sum for the purchase of books for establishing the branches, and for the general management. The Trustees were to be required to make an annual report to the Mayor and City Council of their proceedings and of the condition of the Library, and the report was also to contain a full account of the money received and expended. Mr. Pratt said, in conclusion, that the plan thus proposed for the support and management of the Library was the result of long and careful consideration, and that he was satisfied it was well adapted to promote the great object in view—the free circulation of the books of a large and ever-growing Library among the people of the whole City. Such was Mr. Pratt's generous offer and judicious plan as set forth by himself.

On the 30th of March, 1882, the General Assembly of Maryland passed an act incorporating the Library exactly according to the plan proposed by Mr. Pratt, and also authorizing the Mayor and City Council of Baltimore to pass an ordinance to carry the plan into full effect, provided said ordinance should be approved by a majority of the votes of the people of the City. The necessary ordinance was accordingly passed by the Mayor and City Council of Baltimore on the 15th of July, 1882, and on the 6th of November, 1882, the ordinance was accepted by the vote of the people. These careful and somewhat complicated proceedings on the part of the Mayor and City Council of Baltimore and of the General Assembly of the State, and their ratification by the subsequent vote of the people of the City, were deemed to be expedient, and perhaps necessary, in view of a provision of the Constitution of the State.

The General Assembly of the State of Maryland, in the session of 1882, eloquently expressed in a joint resolution its sense of the beneficence of Mr. Pratt, and of the value of his foundation.

Never in Maryland has a public Institution been founded with so much care and with such hearty approval on the part of the people of Baltimore, and of the constituted authorities of both City and State.

As has been stated, Mr. Pratt contributed the sum of $1,058,000, a portion of which was expended in building and other necessary improvements, and the residue — namely, $833,333.33⅓ — was paid in cash to the City. On this sum the City has agreed to pay interest at the rate of six per cent., or $50,000 annually, for the support of the Library. Six per cent. is in Maryland the interest allowed by law on all debts, unless a different agreement is made between the parties. A large portion of the City's debt still bears interest at that rate. Most damaging consequences would follow if the income of the Library should vary from year to year with the fluctuations in the market-rate of money. Stability is absolutely essential, and the income thus provided is sufficient, but not more than sufficient, for the great object to be accomplished. For every reason it comported with the dignity and self-respect of the City that on such a debt it should pay the legal rate of interest, and this was approved and agreed to, not only by the General Assembly and City Council, but by the people of Baltimore, acting in their sovereign capacity.

Boston, to her great credit, was the first of American cities to establish a free library. According to the second report of her Trustees, made in 1854, the Library, after it had existed for two years, contained 16,221 volumes. The Pratt Library begins with nearly twice as many. The Boston Library, including the branches, has increased to the number of 453,947 volumes, but much the greater part is not for circulation or popular use, but for research and for scholars. In addition to an income from investments generously given by individuals, amounting to about

$7000, Boston, during the last two years, has appropriated each year for the support of her Library $120,000. Her Library buildings have cost the city a large sum of money, and a larger building is now contemplated. Much of this great expense arises not from the circulating and popular feature of the library, but from the department of research and study. This department, as I have already said, is in Baltimore amply provided for by the Library of the Peabody Institute.

There is another consideration which makes a free library especially valuable in this City at this time. For a long period Maryland, in common with her sister States of the South, suffered from the existence of African slavery, now for more than twenty years happily abolished. While slavery lasted it was a hindrance and obstacle to the progress of both races, to those who were free as well as to those who were enslaved. Now Baltimore stands erect, with every weight removed, at the entrance of a free and therefore new South, of which she is a part, and with all the possibilities of intellectual development in which she shares. Already has the genius of Southern people flowered forth with unexpected luxuriance. Sidney Lanier, who came to Baltimore after the close of the Civil War, was soon honorably associated first with the Peabody Institute, and afterwards, until his death, with Johns Hopkins University as Lecturer. The noble purity and simplicity of his life were quickly recognized, and the tablet to his memory placed in Hopkins Hall shows the high estimation in which he was held by the University; but it is only since his death that the published volume of his poems has revealed the subtlety, delicacy and power of his genius. George W. Cable, especially, in his " Old Creole Days," has with singular skill and power opened a new and fascinating region of fiction which seems to belong to himself alone. Joel Chandler Harris, in the wit, wisdom and folk-lore of " Uncle Remus," has won the hearts of young and old. Who has not laughed till he cried over the legend of the " Tar-Baby"? Who does not sympathize with the little boy who, when he saw a dead rabbit, wept bitterly and refused to be comforted, because he said he knew that " Brer Rabbit" was dead at last? And Mary N. Murfree, or Charles Egbert Craddock, as she prefers to be called, has not only made famous her beloved Tennessee mountains, but has accomplished the more difficult task of creating an interest in the rude mountaineers, ennobled as they are in the light of her genius, by heroic and tender traits in both man and woman. We cannot hear in the city streets the coming footsteps of our writers and thinkers. They will appear in their own good time, and will not be hastened at our pleasure; but wherever there is genius it is fostered by books freely offered and freely used. Perhaps we may hope at some time for another genius as bright, but not as wayward, as the poet Edgar Allan Poe, who sleeps in our soil, where he properly belongs, but whose fame is not bounded by the narrow limits of any city or State or country. Free libraries are not made wholly for authors, original thinkers and men of genius, for these must always be few in numbers, but chiefly for those who hunger and thirst, as I believe all intelligent people sometimes do, for something better and higher than the pursuits of the mere workday world in which they live, and to all such the Library, with its books and periodicals, its pleasant reading-rooms, and the instructive or entertaining volumes to be taken away as home companions, is an unspeakable blessing. The invitation is to all. A few love knowledge for its own sake, some from a desire to know the truth, and others for various reasons; but every one who desires to learn something worth knowing, must go for the instruction to the surest source—that is, to the best books. The cordial invitation extended to all seekers for knowledge can hardly be better expressed than in the appeal uttered long ago by the wise son of Sirach. He still says to us, in language which our Library reiterates, "Draw near unto me, ye unlearned, and dwell in the house of learning." There is a much larger class who will resort to this Library, and whose wants should be amply supplied—those who seek for good literature without any definite purpose of study, but for relaxation of mind, for innocent enjoyment, and for general culture. How many there are to-day in this city who are worn down by household cares, by the drudgery of daily toil, and by the anxieties of business! how many by the still greater trials and bereavements which are inseparable incidents of our chequered human existence! To such will come as a benediction the invitation which I would fain borrow from the sweet and tender words of Shakespeare:

> "Come and take choice of all my library,
> And so beguile thy sorrow."

Good literature! What region of thought and feeling does it not embrace? What heart does it not soften? What intellect does it not quicken? What soul does it not elevate? Let me close with an extract from Edgar Quinet, a modern French writer who knew and loved literature well, and who at the close of his career thus expressed his gratitude: "I have profited," he said, "from the days and years which have been given me to live in familiarity with the great minds of all times. Those good geniuses, who have made the world illustrious, have not disdained me. Without demanding of me my titles, who I am, or whence I came, they have admitted me into their company. They have opened to me their volumes; they have allowed me to read into their thoughts, their secrets; they have let me drink of their sweet knowledge. I have forgotten in this occupation the evil days which have come upon me."

ADDRESS OF HON. J. MORRISON HARRIS.

Mr. Pratt, Ladies and Gentlemen:

In view of this thronged and brilliant audience, so largely representing the culture and intelligence of the City, one may well say, "Peace hath her victories no less renowned than war," and that a quiet and unostentatious citizen may achieve a popular triumph, as brilliant as that accorded the successful soldier, by a simple act that illustrates his acceptance of a great idea—the recognition by wealth of the responsibility of wealth. That money is power, is common experience crystallized into proverb. I am not concerned to-day either with the manner of its acquisition or the modes of its abuse. I heartily wish that all who have it may be happy in its possession, and I take it that far too much of the sharp criticism rising into bitter denunciation of the rich, because they fail to do the many things we think they ought to do, and are sure we would do in their places, has in it very positive elements of injustice, self-deception and humbug.

There are, however, phases of the subject in which you and I, leaving to others the cheap luxury of condemnation, have a right both to speak and feel. These are the occasions when the millions are brought in contact with the wants and interests of the many, and the immense leverage of money applied to the relief, instruction and elevation of the masses of the people, making lighter the burdens of poverty, softening the asperities of adverse fortune, leading ignorance into light, stimulating the honorable ambition of willing labor, developing and fostering true manliness, and, through the thousand channels into which the dedicated wealth may be turned, bringing comfort and health and happiness to multitudes dwelling in the deserts and choked with the sands of life.

Wisely, willingly and cordially we greet the men who so use their abundant wealth, for they have well deserved our acclamations of praise.

The free-library endowment interests me chiefly because it plants in the community another educational force. I believe in and advocate popular education widely diffused and free as it is possible to make it; not as the luxury of the few, but as the primary and essential need of the many, underlying and presupposed by our political theory. We need it on all wise lines and through all legitimate agencies. We want it by public legislation and by private munificence. We want it on the lines of the judicious curriculum, the intelligent and absolutely non-political and non-sectarian administration of a liberally sustained public-school system. We want it on the lines of the Free Library, such as you, sir, have given us, with its seat in the centre of population and its arms reaching out to the circumference, with its doors open to all, and its treasures of instruction to be availed of, I trust, by ever-increasing multitudes as the years roll on. We want it through the opportunities of a Library of scholarly reference and research, and we want it on the yet broader lines of a great University, where studious labor and intellectual fitness may receive thorough equipment, grasp the large problems of philosophy, trace the devious course of history, and in the limitless fields of scientific research make brilliant discovery of new and sublime truths.

Largely as these wants have been met by the munificence of Peabody, Hopkins and Pratt, the need is not wholly fulfilled.

We have, indeed, great reason to be proud of these comparatively new departures on the line of the City's truest progress, and, in connection with them, of the very well-sustained institutions that evidence the abundant interest of our people in the relief of suffering, misfortune and want—noble institutions that stretch forth hands of benediction over the city, and the mainspring of whose vitality and utility is in the warm hearts, earnest faith and unstinted labor of sympathetic woman. Estimating, however, at the highest the value and results of the Peabody Institute and the Hopkins University, we may still feel that by reason of actual—it may be necessary—limitations there are large classes of our fellow-citizens who derive from these great endowments a general rather than immediate and special benefit. To the needs of these the free school and Free Library must minister, and thoughtful men will admit that the service they are competent to render touches nearly and certainly the interests of the community at large. It is late in the day to argue against the curse of illiteracy or seek to prove the close alliance of ignorance and vice. We do not go back to the dawn to seek the source of light with the sun blazing at meridian; and while it would be folly to insist that education will make men saints, we may not deny its influence in the formation of character and the more intelligent appreciation and maintenance of civil rights.

If it stops here and secures only these results, it has done much for the common good; but it goes further and accomplishes more. It is not enough that the classes to which I refer should be made more intelligent as citizens; they should be made happy as men; they, too, should have their share of the best. They have homes, and the sanctities of the fireside are crowned with a purer influence, and the ties of family unite them with a more sacred bond, in the degree that their homes are made attractive and happy. To teach them and their children to read is a point gained, but it needs to be supplemented by something to read.

Some people think that the value and delight

of books are a sort of perquisite of the more fortunate classes, just as others assume that the rich alone are the helpers of the poor. They are mistaken in both conclusions. The instant helpers of the poor are the poor; it may be a broken crust or a shared fagot, but so it is; and by none is a suitable book more eagerly grasped than by those who are unable to buy one. There are faculties and aspirations that are God's endowment of our common humanity, and they are fortunate co-workers who labor to lift the veil that shrouds and pierce the environment that clogs their development.

In view of the dependence and interdependence of human relations, it is always well that wealth and influence should regard with kindly consideration the classes that need help; but there are times when circumstances emphasize the peculiar wisdom of forbearance and justice. I open no discussion and enter into no details inappropriate to the occasion; but observant men cannot fail to see the clouds gathering on the horizon and hear the sounds ominous of storm, or to realize that to-day there are questions that must have answer, and problems for which safe solution must be found.

I advocate, further, the need and value of education in connection with a special class in our midst—a large and meritorious one, worthy of help because always self-helping. I mean our mechanics; and in their case, the higher training I would urge gives promise of outcome in positive relation to the interests of the whole community. The demand of the times and the pressure of competition require that the labor of these artisans, artificers, operatives, these workers with machinery and instruments, should be skilled labor, and their training should be special, direct and practical, tending to their systematic knowledge of the theory and practice of the industrial arts, and so far an art education bearing upon the results to be attained, in obedience to the great principle that intelligence is the most important element of progress in every department of industry. In all the leading European nations, concurrently with the mobilization of armies and the greed of conquest, spurred by pride and urged in the interests of national aggrandizement, an earnest struggle is being made for industrial supremacy—the great prize of industrial education; and this struggle enlists the gravest interest of statesmen and thinkers alike, because they realize that national wealth and prosperity rest on the enlightened employment of natural products and forces, and that national advancement is best secured by promoting the intellectual development of their industrial population. Hence, in England, Germany, France, Belgium and elsewhere, schools for special training in industrial arts are constantly multiplying, while this country, with a people keen, capable and energetic, and a wealth of natural resources almost incalculable, has scarcely entered into the great competition. Herein lies the unfulfilled need to which I before referred. Here is the splendid opportunity for another generous endowment. We need an industrial-art school, a technological institute, wherein labor may be trained into skill and skill make return in profit and honor; wherein our young men may be armed for contest on fair terms upon the field of this great struggle, and women, crushed and despondent under the burdens of life, may be fitted for suitable occupations in which industry and taste will lead to reputation and emolument. I may be oversanguine, but I have faith in my idea, and I have abiding confidence in the force of example. Like begets like, and great endowments for noble purposes have followed each other in this community with a rapidity for which we ourselves were hardly prepared, and at the hint of which our grandfathers would have been smitten with great amazement. We have outlived the day and the thought of our grandfathers.

I recall occasions when I was present at conversations between the late Johns Hopkins and Mr. John W. Garrett—my personal relations with the latter of whom for many years, will always be to me matter of gratification and pride—one of which occurred at the time of the last visit of George Peabody to the Institute he had so generously founded, and where he received a popular ovation honorable to the multitude who so heartily tendered it, and the City in which his name will always be honored. The conversation naturally turned to Mr. Peabody—what he had done and the deep impression made by his liberal act; and I remember Mr. Garrett, turning to Mr. Hopkins, said: "You will have to do something like this with your money. You are a bachelor, and after dealing as liberally as you wish for every one you care to provide for, you will have to leave a great estate behind you before long. You will have to think over something on a large scale." I do not recall what Mr. Hopkins said, probably because he made no special reply. At another time, when I talked over with Mr. Garrett the affairs of the Young Men's Christian Association, for whose building fund I was anxious to obtain subscriptions, and to the agreement for which he had put his own name for ten thousand dollars, he said: "Now you go and talk to Mr. Hopkins—I have already done so—and he will give you something." I went, and he subscribed the same sum. Later, I learned that he had been considering a project on the line of the conversation referred to—the establishment, I think, of a line of steamers to Brazil. What influence other than that Mr. Garrett sedulously brought to bear suggested the great uses to which he finally devoted the bulk of his estate, I do not know; but I am convinced that to the influence of his old friend and constant adviser we are largely indebted for the ultimate dedication of his wealth, the fruits of which we now, and generations to come, will enjoy.

So much for personal influence and the value of example. And let us not forget that when the friendly adviser came to deal with his own wealth, and, full of years and crowned with honor, prepared to lay it down—that while he fulfilled all the obligations of family, he made princely provision for wise and benevolent uses by an unrestricted bequest of six thousand dollars every year to the Poor Association of the city, and a gift of $50,000 to be dispensed annually for "charitable, educational and other purposes of public utility, calculated to promote the happiness, usefulness and progress of society"—and this magnificent provision not limited to the present generation, but running on to the grandchildren of the giver.

Passing for a moment from what has been accomplished in our midst upon these lines of special and general education, and the enlarged benefits to which we may reasonably look in the near future, I would say a word, before closing, of the incalculable value, sovereign influence and exquisite delight of books; how they store the chambers of memory and strengthen the fibres of mind; how they bridge the chasms of the past, illumine the present and mould the future; and how with them we pass from the vagueness of tradition into the light of history, grow familiar with the greatness of individual lives, the crystallizations of society, the growth and decadence of organized empire, the convulsions of war and the arts of peace; and, tracing the flow and reflux of civilization and progress, see its long-fretted and obstructed current widen into the assured breadth and sweep of this, its century of triumphant development. Only by retrospection and introspection do we conceive adequately how much we owe to these multiform digests of the experience and thought of time and the world—these full arsenals to which we go alike for the weapons that arm us for the conflicts, and the contentment that soothes us in the disappointments of life.

Doubtless there are worthless and dangerous books that tempt the unwary and mislead the weak; that build up false philosophies and inculcate evil morals; that degrade science by the assumptions of ignorance, and dishonor religion by the bitterness of dogmatism; that touch with doubting finger the holiest shrines of faith, and sap the securest foundations of society; but where the few infuse the poison the many bring the antidote, and to-day we go to the printed book for the overthrow of error, rather than to the limited refutation of the pulpit or the ephemeral discussion of the rostrum.

The complete library ministers to all wants, satisfies all tastes, meets all inquiries. It is the cosmos of mind, the epitome of knowledge. It aids the profoundest thinker, and stimulates the simplest reader. It gives the politician the principles and examples of statesmanship, inflames the ardor and illustrates the nobility of patriotism. With its "gift of tongues" it speaks in all languages to all nationalities. In it imagination finds exaltation, and labor learns skill. There are the flaming chariots of genius and the white sails of adventure, and there are revealed the majestic procession of natural forces and the omnipresent laws of divine control.

Upon books rest the promise and security of all progress, material, intellectual, religious; of all science, invention, art; of all rights, government order; of all convenience, comfort, happiness; and so, touching each arc of the rounded circle of personal, political and social life, with them all possibilities of civilization await us in the future, while without them man's lapse into barbarism, though gradual, would be sure.

And now, sir (addressing Mr. Pratt), there is left me the great pleasure of uniting with the mass of your fellow-citizens in expressing the general appreciation of your noble act, that, while illustrating your high and unselfish spirit, shows that you have met with warm sympathy and wise prevision one of the great needs of our people, and have very wisely carried out your purpose while living. I do not doubt that the successful and beneficent working of your Library will be a source of great happiness to you in the many years we all hope you will continue to realize it, with the added satisfaction of anticipating the blessing it will prove to multitudes who will succeed those who now applaud you; to be enhanced, I trust, by the pleasant consciousness that others, affected by your example, have also entered these lists of honor.

ADDRESS OF HON. FERDINAND C. LATROBE, EX-MAYOR OF BALTIMORE.

Ladies and Gentlemen :—In presenting a free library to the city, Mr. Pratt has the satisfaction of knowing that he will give pleasure, instruction and knowledge not only to his fellow-citizens, but to all those who will live here after us. He will know that the people are bettered by his liberality, that he adds another to our monuments—not an inspiring shaft of marble, or statue of bronze, commemorating fame or patriotism, but a storehouse from whose shelves will flow that knowledge which, with mercy, is "like the gentle rain from heaven, blessing him who gives and him who takes." The stream for which he has furnished the inexhaustible supply will continue through coming generations, who will remember his name as long as Baltimore does last. If I may be permitted to say it in his presence, the wisdom, shrewdness and business sagacity which enable him to exercise this liberality are indicated by the fact that it is not a post-mortem bequest, but given in that full tide of life and health which we hope he may long enjoy, and when he can himself witness some of those blessings which we are told belong more to the giver than to the recipient. The acquisition of large wealth is no easy matter, or more of us would have it; it represents labor, industry, energy, tact, economy, and a little of what is called good fortune, or, at least, opportunity. Being difficult to win, it is generally hard to willingly part with. One power alone absolutely takes it away—death. Therefore, he who gives without that final compulsion, gives freely, and, by witnessing the good resulting from his gift, secures at least a personal gratification from his own liberality. We desire that Mr. Pratt may fully realize how much his gift to Baltimore is appreciated. That the Library will be of practical benefit there is no doubt. Each year demonstrates the advantages of free public education. The yearning for learning is engrafted in the nature of American citizens. Believing in the equality of the people, insisting that no man or woman is confined by birth to one class of society—in other words, that "all men are born free and equal"—and having won the acknowledgment of these, as we claim natural, rights, we know they can be withheld only by force of arms or loss of educated intelligence. The former we do not fear, and the latter, far more dangerous, we are determined to guard against. It is admitted by wise statesmen that political liberty rests upon the foundation-stone of free public education. The free schoolhouse is, therefore, regarded as a necessity with those who love republican institutions, and the people submit without murmuring to heavy taxation for its maintenance.

But the schoolhouse is only on the threshold of the temple of knowledge. What those who have left the school-desk require is books to make available the desire for knowledge acquired in the public school—free books within the reach of every one of the 40,000 children who annually attend the public schools of Baltimore. We give with free education free books for tuition, but we had no Free Library to furnish the necessary supplement for that necessity, "free schools." It is this Free Library that Mr. Enoch Pratt has given us, at a cost of over one million dollars. For it, this large audience, representing the intelligence and patriotism of Baltimore, has assembled to say, "Mr. Pratt, we thank you."

ADDRESS OF DR. LEWIS H. STEINER, LIBRARIAN.

Ladies and Gentlemen:—Your presence at the opening exercises of the Free Library shows your appreciation of the advantages which are expected to be derived from its establishment, and how grateful you feel towards the generous founder whose name it bears. I congratulate you, the Board of Trustees, and Mr. Pratt, that, the days of preparation being over, on the morrow the doors of the Central Library will be thrown open to every anxious seeker after knowledge, without respect to rank, condition or color, and that all will have the opportunity, then and thenceforth, to avail themselves of the constantly increasing number of silent instructors which will be at the disposal of every one in this people's university. I congratulate you, citizens of Baltimore, on the introduction of another instrumentality for the increase and diffusion of knowledge and culture in your midst, in addition to those that have of late years so largely contributed to the reputation of the City. And I trust that I may also be allowed to felicitate myself upon this formal establishment of such relations with you as will enable me to execute the high trust committed to me, so as to secure the greatest good to the greatest number of the community.

"Ideas once generated live forever," says an old writer. But, in order that these may undergo normal development and healthy growth, they must be planted in favorable soil and supplied with such external conditions as will insure the fullest development of their possibilities and potentialities. So long as the brilliant conceptions of genius remain locked up in the brains of their authors, so long as the suggestion of a new application of the forces of Nature lingers concealed in the mind of the inventor, so long as a profound thought is kept from contact with the active, busy world of thinkers, inventors and practical men who may make it useful, so long it is but a lifeless seed, unable to grow, develop and bear rich fruit. Hence the necessity for some means of communicating the thoughts of others so as to make them the common property of mankind. They must be placed where they can contribute to the good of the race, and be supplied with the conditions that will allow them to furnish perennial proof of the undying life they possess.

Before the invention of printing, efforts were made to accomplish this by oral communication, or by the slow written multiplication of statements of the truths that man, having discovered, was willing to make the common property of his fellow-man. The former was a very unreliable method of securing accuracy of transmission, and the latter cumbrous and expensive;

but when printing was discovered, then the thoughts of the wise were enshrined in a permanent shape that might be seized and appropriated as his own by whomsoever it was appreciatively read and lovingly taken to heart. The readers of books, necessarily, at first were a very limited class, and were disposed to conceal themselves modestly from a world which was busied with agriculture, commerce, war, and the intricate stratagems that seem inseparable from monarchical governments. But the people began to thirst after some of the intellectual enjoyment that seemed peculiar to this class. They grew restive under the yoke of slavery. The heaven-born aspirations implanted in every human breast impelled them to pry into the mysteries of knowledge, to seek for the key that would unlock its storehouses, to make an acquaintance with those great ideas, truths, and even facts, which were apparently stored away in printed pages. Students sprang up from all classes of society—largely, be it said, with laudable pride, from the masses rather than the nobility; ideas that had lain dormant began to swell with a life that brought practical science and invention to the front; the test of practical worth, rather than that of accidental association or unavoidable descent, began to be applied to men, and the race actually started out on a new course with a life and energy never dreamed of before by its most hopeful sons.

The ministry of books had been invoked. The art that Faust and Gutenberg and Koster had given to mankind was now enlisted in the service of human advancement. From cloister and cell, where truths had been carefully stored away for centuries in precious manuscripts, knowledge came forth and was lovingly greeted by those who had longed for an acquaintance with its treasures. The brotherhood of man and the equality of all the sons of men before the law then began to assert themselves as truths of primeval origin which had been lying dormant through countless ages. There was restlessness under despotism, and dissatisfaction with government not springing from the consent of the governed. These grew and strengthened until they asserted themselves here in their mightiest form—in the establishment of a republic where each should stand the equal of the other, and *worth* alone should be entitled to the respect and reverence that had been previously paid to circumstances which were accidents in the individual.

If we would be true to our duty and properly grateful for the blessings which the printed page has brought to us and our homes, we must strive to bring the ministry of books to our fellow-men. This is acknowledged by the advocates of popular education on all sides. Hence the public, when it is sufficiently enlightened to understand the subject, submits cheerfully to a fair taxation, in order that schools may be established for all classes, and the blessings of rudimentary education may be made as free as the air of heaven or the water of the sea. In this city, under wise and prudent educators, a system of public schools has been established and developed, until it now occupies the proud position of being among the best in the United States. But its advantages only arouse and stimulate a thirst for knowledge which must be satisfied in some other way. Those who have completed the requisite curriculum of the schools can no longer rest contented with the *quasi*-vegetative life that satisfies him who is altogether devoid of intellectual culture; those who have been allowed only a taste at the Pierian spring will—if opportunity is but allowed them—hasten forward to drink deeper and still deeper draughts of life-giving knowledge.

Where shall such opportunities be secured? How shall the wants of the masses, first excited and developed in the schools, be supplied? It is not only the favored student who has, in college or university, sat under the teachings of mature wisdom, that feels the need of the ministry of books when his days of pupilage are over. His humbler and less favored brother has the same earnest longing and seeks the same relief. Here the value of a free public library asserts itself. It brings to the people the opportunity of supplementing whatever knowledge may have been acquired in the schools with the glowing thoughts and burning words of the best writers and greatest thinkers. It places every one on a broad platform of democratic equality such as only has a right to any recognition in the republic of letters. It is the true people's university, where all may read, learn, imbibe and appropriate the results of the thought and study of those who have occupied chairs of instruction in the higher schools, and such as have unselfishly devoted their lives to extending the boundaries of knowledge. The free library and the learned university have the same ultimate objects in view—viz.: the elevation of the race, its advancement along the lines of culture, and its progressive victory over the trammels of Time and Nature. They dare not antagonize. Each must assist and help the other. Even now, as in the enthusiastic glow that animates us at the inauguration of the *one* which we hope will be of priceless value to Baltimore, we dare not forget that the *other*—inaugurated not quite ten years ago in this very Academy, and whose faculty honors these ceremonies with their presence—has never been content with the mere attainment of recognition from the learned world, but has always been ready to aid in any enterprise promising to benefit popular culture in the City where it is located. Long may they labor, each in its own sphere, for the diffusion of the blessings of human knowledge!

Fellow-citizens, the temptation to speak more at length is great, but I must close. A few words more and the part assigned to me will have been performed. On to-morrow—Tuesday—morning, the issue of books at the Central Library, to those who have secured library cards, will take place, to continue, we hope, as long as the City endures. The Library practically belongs to the citizens of Baltimore. The preservation of its books from injury is an object of importance to every citizen. We invoke your assistance in this regard. You have already shown scrupulous care of the beautiful shrubbery and flowers that adorn your public squares. May we not expect still greater care in reference to the buildings and books that have been so generously donated for your use and that of your children?

Twenty thousand volumes have been collected for the Central Library; twelve thousand more will be placed, within a few weeks, on the shelves of its branches. Yearly additions will be made to these. Starting under auspicious circumstances, may we not trust that this Library and its branches shall, under the enlightened and wise management of its Trustees, with the blessing of that kind Providence who placed the thought of establishing it in the heart of the founder, be the means of making our City and our State wiser, greater and better, and that future generations will bless the name of him who so bountifully provided for the intellectual wants of his fellow-men?

THE CENTRAL LIBRARY BUILDING.

The Main or Central Library Building is situated on Mulberry near Cathedral street. It (together with the four Branch Buildings) was designed and the construction superintended by Mr. Chas. L. Carson, architect. It has a frontage of eighty-two feet, and a depth of one hundred and forty feet to a twenty-foot alley, and is thoroughly fire-proof in construction throughout. The building is treated in the bold Romanesque style, with its characteristic semicircular forms, relief mouldings, enriched carvings and embellishments. The façade, from the ground line to and including the cornice, is constructed of Baltimore County white marble, tool-dressed to an even surface, with polished granite pillars and pilasters supporting arched windows. In the centre of the front a tower rises to the height of ninety-eight feet, and clearly designates and marks the main entrance, vestibule and staircase hall. On each side of this tower are clustered three large semicircular-headed windows, over which, and in line with the second floor, there is an enriched moulded cornice. Above this point the two wings (east and west) are treated differently as to arrangement of openings. The east wing being three stories, and the west wing but two stories in height

and they are designed so as to come within one level cornice line at the roof, thereby presenting evenness of sky lines broken only by the tower. In the upper story of the tower there is an artistically carved allegorical panel in bas-relief representing History, and in the east and west wings on each side of the tower, in spandrels formed by the circular window-heads, there are five medallion full-relief busts of eminent authors and artists, modelled and carved out of Italian statuary marble. Other appropriate enrichments are introduced in proper places, and evenly distributed throughout the building, which, with the general treatment and outline, are designed to produce a feeling of earnestness and repose.

The building is entered by a large centre doorway ten feet wide. Heavy carved oaken doors, the inner pair having cathedral glass in large panels, swing back, disclosing exquisite tints in enamel tiles, which cover the walls above the wainscoting, in buff, blue, chocolate, white, black and brown. The floor of the vestibule is laid with marble in black and white. The wainscoting is of Tennessee and Vermont marbles, principally of a dove-color. A graceful arch of Cheat River blue sandstone faces the entrance, supported by two columns of Tennessee marble, of the tint known as " maiden's blush." The bases of the columns are of black Irish marble. The stairway of marble is broad and easy, and is constructed of Italian treads and maiden's-blush risers, upon a framework of iron. The balustrade is massive, but in excellent proportions. The balusters are of bronze, with a mahogany rail. The newel-post is a block of dove-colored marble, from which rises an elegant bronze gas fixture.

The room to the right, thirty feet square and twenty feet high, is for the delivery of books. This room is the one most frequented by the people, and the one where borrowers must wait till the books called for can be brought from the shelves and charged to them. It is provided with an open fireplace, and a large heated ventilating flue, four feet by fourteen inches, runs directly through to the roof in an inner wall, to keep the air pure during the business hours of the day. A counter runs the entire length of the room. The floor is of marble, the woodwork of old oak with antique chimneypieces, etc. A window for books and a door for attendants open into the large book room behind, and a small lift extends to the upper stories for ready and safe transit of books.

On the left of the vestibule is another room, of the same size, for the return of books, finished in the same style and of the same materials. This room is also connected with the great book rooms and with the delivery room. Behind these front rooms are the two large book rooms, arranged one above the other in two half stories, each room seventy-five feet long, thirty-seven feet wide, and nine feet high, the building being drawn in twenty feet on each side to furnish light and air. Shelves crossing each of these rooms from east to west divide it into fifteen alcoves five feet wide, and every alcove is lighted by a window at each end of it. Passageways three feet wide run north and south along the walls and through the centre of the rooms. No books are placed on the outer walls. The two stories are connected by iron stairs and lifts for the easy and rapid transmission of books to the delivery room. The floors of both book rooms are laid with iron plates, and the windows provided with iron shutters on the inside. These rooms will hold 150,000 volumes. At the top of the marble stairway, in the vestibule, is a spacious hall, paved and wainscoted with marble, and lighted by a large window of stained glass. In the southwest corner of the second story on Mulberry street is a suite of rooms for the Trustees, consisting of a large meeting-room, a smaller committee room, and suitable offices.

But the grand feature of the building is the reading-room. It is placed in the second story, directly over the two book rooms and at the head of the grand stairway, and is seventy-five feet long, thirty-seven feet wide and twenty-five feet high. The walls are frescoed in buff and pale green tints, the ceiling is heavily panelled, with rich gilt moulding tracing the cornice, the wainscoting is of Lisbon, Irish and Tennessee marble, the floor is inlaid with cherry, pine and oak, and over the windows are circular transoms in stained glass bearing the portraits of Bryant, Pope, Scott, Dante, Molière, Byron, Goethe, Shakespeare, Schiller and Milton. Eight pure brass gas fixtures, two with twelve burners and the others with six, afford a brilliant light. There are ten large windows—five on each side—set five feet from the floor to admit a flood of light from above—the most agreeable light possible for reading. It is provided with two large ventilating flues to secure a constant supply of pure air, even when the room shall be occupied by the 250 readers that it will accommodate. A long desk is placed in the south-east corner of the room, near the entrance door. This desk is connected by a stairway with the book rooms below, and by a door with another large book room directly over the delivery room. This latter room is situated in the southeast corner of the building, on the Mulberry street front, is thirty feet square, is divided into two stories of nine feet each, and will hold 50,000 volumes. While this room is designed especially to accommodate the reading-room which adjoins it, and will contain maps, books of reference, and such other works as will be most used in that room, it is rendered conveniently accessible by stairs and a lift to the delivery room below it. Space is thus provided for the safe and convenient storage of 200,000 volumes of books. Besides these four rooms, there are two others in the basement that can be fitted with shelves in case of need, and the walls of the Librarian's room and the work room can be lined with them. Ample accommodation will thus be afforded for 250,000 volumes, but the building was planned for only 200,000 volumes; and this number its three book rooms will hold without crowding.

North of the reading-room and the two principal book rooms the building again expands for twenty feet into a width of seventy-six feet, and extends back to a twenty-foot alley. This portion of the edifice contains the janitor's apartments; a room for receiving and unpacking the boxes of new books, and for packing and sending off books to the Branch Libraries; a room for repairing books injured by use; a work room for recording and cataloguing new books, and preparing them for the shelves; a Librarian's room; separate lavatories and other offices for male and female attendants; a large chimney to be utilized in ventilation; stairways (of iron), and a large lift extending from the cellar up through all the stories. It will be seen that the reading-room occupies the centre of the lot, and is separated both from Mulberry street and the back alley by the wider intervening parts of the building. It is thus removed from the noise of both streets—an important gain for undisturbed reading and quiet study. This Library Building has been planned with the utmost care, after long and careful study of the needs of such a structure and the conveniences required in it, and after an examination and study of the important libraries of the world. The aim has been to provide storage for 200,000 volumes of books; to render these volumes easily accessible to the delivery room, to the returning room and to the reading-room; to provide a convenient, comfortable, light, cheerful and healthful reading-room, with accommodations for not less than 200 readers, and to provide all other rooms necessary for the accommodation of the borrowers of books, the Trustees, the Librarian, the janitor, and all the attendants of both sexes required in such an establishment; rooms for the reception of new books, and for the transfer of books to and from the Branches.

THE BRANCH BUILDINGS.

The four Branch Buildings are located in the northwestern, southwestern, southern and extreme eastern portions of the City, and are of uniform architecture. They are each forty by seventy feet, one story in height; with a high, well lighted basement; are built of Baltimore pressed brick laid with red mortar, with buff Dorchester stone trimmings. The style of architecture is Romanesque; the treatment bold and striking. The elaborate terra-cotta moulded panels, the quaint high peaked slate roof with "eye-brow" windows, though not so imposing as the Central Building, yet being unique in general appearance, they present a pleasing architectural feature in the different localities where situated. The location of each has been carefully studied; and the buildings being on prominent thoroughfares and at the intersection of streets, will continue to be prominent landmarks, and reflect the sagacity of the founder, who not only provided the citizens of Baltimore with the best and most carefully selected reading matter, but brought it to their very doors. These buildings have a large hall, with one high open-timbered story finished to the roof. At the end of this hall is the counter for issuing and receiving books. Opening into this is a large reading room; the partition of opaque glass above the wainscoting separating the two, extending only to the height of the square of the building, allowing free circulation of air and light. The reading-room is finished in light wood, and amply lighted and ventilated. The book room (with shelving for fifteen thousand volumes), and the Librarian's work room, etc., etc., occupy the rear end of the building. In the interior finish—of hard wood—and the decorations, the harmony of colors used, the enamelled brick interior of the vestibule, the stained glass windows, antique brass gas fixtures, etc., the Branch Buildings are especially well adapted to the purposes for which they are designed, and an atmosphere of quiet comfort and repose pervades their precincts that is particularly attractive to the student or the lover of good literature. A supply of periodicals is kept at the Branches, and the reading room is furnished with the latest lexicons, encyclopædias, and other books of general reference.

A SKETCH OF THE FOUNDER.

Enoch Pratt was born in North Middleborough, Massachusetts, September 10th, 1808. He is the son of Isaac and Naomi (Keith) Pratt. His father's record, and that of his ancestors, is well known in the North. He graduated at Bridgewater Academy at the age of fifteen. Two weeks before he closed his term at the Academy, he wrote a letter to an intimate friend of his family in Boston to obtain for him as soon as possible a good place in a wholesale dry goods house. He said: "I suspect that I am old enough to do considerable business. . . . . The preceptor thinks that I am. . . . . My school will be out in a fortnight, and I do not want to stay at home long after it is out." A position was soon secured for him in a first-class house in Boston, where he remained until he was twenty-one years of age. In this place he had the benefits of the old-fashioned training in business peculiar to Boston, and the influence of the examples of good men to aid him in developing those traits of character which have distinguished him from boyhood to manhood, and through life. His unexceptionable habits and tireless application to business; his quick perception of what was right and what was wrong, and his undeviating integrity; the simplicity of his method, and his unbounded confidence in the principles of common sense, and in the results of legitimate industry, gave him an early reputation for sound judgment of far greater value than the possession of money as a capital, with its dangerous tendency to mislead in the choice of doubtful projects of speculation. The slow and sure methods of acquisition afford the most profitable information in respect to the fundamental laws of trade and the means of success. No young man more thoroughly mastered these laws and observed them than the subject of this notice.

In 1831 Mr. Pratt removed to Baltimore, and established himself as a commission merchant. He founded the wholesale iron house of Pratt & Keith and subsequently that of Enoch Pratt & Brother, which latter now consists of himself and his brother-in-law, Henry Janes. No firms have been more successful in business, though much of the time of Mr. Pratt has been given to industrial enterprises of a public nature, and to financial institutions. He has been Director and President of the National Farmers' and Planters' Bank for forty-five years; Director and Vice-President of the Philadelphia, Wilmington and Baltimore Railroad for twenty-seven years; also President or Director of numerous other institutions. In the early history of railroads, he identified himself closely with the Philadelphia, Wilmington and Baltimore, as well as with other railroads and steamboat lines connecting with Baltimore or the South. During his residence of fifty-five years in Baltimore, Mr. Pratt has devoted not only his means largely, but his energy and talents to all enterprises of a public nature that have been projected, having for their object the commercial or industrial advancement of the city. His capital and encouragement have been extended to many of the various manufacturing industries in our midst, as he recognized the great importance of the development of domestic manufactures, while not neglecting the establishment of new and better highways for our commerce, both foreign and domestic.

He is now President of the House of Reformation (for Colored Children), at Cheltenham, Prince George's County, and of the Maryland School for the Deaf and Dumb, at Frederick. To the success of both Institutions he contributed largely of his own private means. Mr. Pratt has also taken a lively interest in the Maryland Institute for the Promotion of the Mechanic Arts. The costly bell and clock in the tower of the Institute building were his gift. As the Treasurer of the Peabody Institute, he was highly complimented, by the late eminent banker who founded it, as one of the ablest financiers he had ever known. The ease and success with which he conducted the great trust of millions without loss, and with a skill to secure all possible legitimate gains, afford a singular contrast to modern examples of administrative weakness. In 1877 he was unanimously elected by the City Council one of the Finance Commissioners of the City, a post of honor and great responsibility. This was truly a high compliment, for the reason that he was not a member of the political party then in power. His services as Commissioner proved to be invaluable in shaping the financial policy of the municipality.

The pressure of his private interests, however, induced him after a time to withdraw from this position.

One of his colleagues at that time was the Hon. James Hodges, now Mayor of Baltimore.

Soon after the induction of Mr. Hodges into office, the City Council, with great unanimity, elected Mr. Pratt again to the position of Finance Commissioner, which office he now holds. This compliment, entirely unsolicited and unexpected, was paid to Mr. Pratt in recognition of his former services to the City in the same position, and as a tribute to his ability and long experience as a financier and a citizen to whom Baltimore owes much.

With this exception, Mr. Pratt has uniformly declined all overtures from the citizens of Baltimore or the State of Maryland to hold any political office, although frequently urged strongly to allow his name to be used in such a connection.

But in favoring his adopted city, Mr. Pratt did not forget his native town in Massachusetts. In 1867 he endowed an academy in North Middleborough with the sum of $30,000, and made it free to children within a certain distance. In 1858, when the Congregational church of Titicut was burned, he aided them to rebuild, and presented them with a clock and bell.

Of his happy domestic relations, it may be proper to add that he was married August 1st, 1837, to a most estimable lady, Maria Louisa Hyde, whose paternal ancestors were among the earliest settlers of Massachusetts, while on the mother's side she is descended from a German family which located in Baltimore more than a hundred and fifty years ago. The circle of his home, whether large or small, is made as happy as the means of wealth can command, and the presence of a noble and cheerful mind can inspire.

Mr. Pratt is in the full possession of mental and physical vigor, and is enjoying, without display or ostentation, the rewards of an unspotted career and a life of unclouded prosperity. His large fortune has been accumulated entirely by the labor of his own hands, and is the direct result of a tireless industry and the application of strict integrity and fixedness of purpose to acquire and a wise economy and sagacity to save. When he left his Northern home to seek his fortune in Baltimore he had not a dollar at his command. During his long commercial career he has studiously avoided engaging in speculation of any kind, however alluringly presented; confining himself strictly to the slow gains from the channels of legitimate trade, thus avoiding the rocks upon which so many hopes and fortunes have been wrecked.

No man is more unassuming in his manners, or more modest in speaking of what he has done, or of his personal merits. It cannot be seen that good fortune adds to his vanity, or good deeds to his pride, or that occasional losses annoy him. He dislikes flattery and unnecessary ceremony, and in his intercourse with his neighbors and friends he has a kind and ready greeting for all classes, uttered with an unchangeable dignity that is the natural language of high motives and undisguised sincerity.

In his religious views Mr. Pratt is an eclectic, believing in the rule of God, and finding good in all things. His scale of duty is not measured to time, and in his acts of to-day he religiously provides for the future. He is an active member of the Unitarian Society of Baltimore; but he looks for a man's religion in his deeds. He may be spoken of, in the language of Tennyson, as one

> Whose faith has centre everywhere,
> Nor cares to fix itself to form.

www.ingramcontent.com/pod-product-compliance
Lightning Source LLC
Chambersburg PA
CBHW021940160426
43195CB00011B/1167